RAY FRENCH'S
100
GREAT
RUGBY LEAGUE
PLAYERS

RAY FRENCH'S
100
GREAT
RUGBY LEAGUE
PLAYERS

Macdonald
Queen Anne Press

A Queen Anne Press BOOK

© Ray French

First published in Great Britain in 1989 by
Queen Anne Press, a division of
Macdonald & Co (Publishers) Ltd
Headway House
66–73 Shoe Lane
London
EC4P 4AB

A member of Maxwell Pergamon
Publishing Corporation Ltd

British Library Cataloguing in Publication Data

French, Ray
    Ray French's 100 great rugby league players.
    1. Great Britain. Rugby league football. Players –
    Biographies
    I. Title
    796.33′3′0922

    ISBN 0-356-17578-2

Typeset, printed and bound by Butler & Tanner Ltd, Frome, Somerset

CONTENTS

INTRODUCTION

The immensity of my task in choosing the men who have been the 100 greatest Rugby League players since the code broke away from the ranks of the Rugby Union in 1895 and spawned a game which created its own heroes and legends can be seen in my agonising deliberations before my final choice.

My first reflections on a dark winter's evening left me with 250 names pencilled in as being worthy of inclusion, but also with a feeling that I might be better qualified to attempt the Indian Rope Trick, such seemed the impossibility of my task. Further deliberation helped me to whittle the numbers down to 100 but only after the greatest soul searching and the most difficult decisions. Obviously, as with any sporting selections, there are areas of disagreement and I am certain that my choices will provoke much heated argument but, whatever the discussions, they do remain firmly as my 100 greatest Rugby League players for reasons which I am convinced made or make them superior to all others.

Some of the players in my collection may not have established the records that others did, or not attracted the same amount of media attention but all were, or are, in Rugby League vernacular, 'players' players'. They are respected for their talents by the most crucial and perceptive members of the Rugby League fraternity – the players themselves.

Many are players of yesteryear whom I was unfortunate never to play with or watch, but, after speaking to those who did and after research into their deeds, it is obvious that these players stood out above their contemporaries and, more importantly, they often proved the yardstick by which to assess those who followed in the later decades. Many of my selected players are important not only for their rugby talents but because they often influenced rule changes or were themselves brought to prominence by rule changes. Others changed the direction and welfare of the League code by their attitudes both on and off the field. All have charisma, and, whatever their weaknesses, at their best there were few to equal them in what they did best. Rugby League is a sport which, at the professional level, depends for its livelihood and future on the paying spectator and, on that basis alone, all my players were worthy of selection because they enhanced the game they loved by being, simply, entertainers.

Neil Fox, Eric Ashton, Mick
Sullivan and Billy Boston
played together in seven
Tests in 1961 and 1962 to
make one of the most
awesome threequarter lines in
the history of Rugby League.

JACK ARKWRIGHT

b. 3.12.1902
St Helens, Warrington,
Great Britain

Many Union stars sign Rugby League registration forms for thousands of pounds, schoolboys often turn to the game for a few hundred pounds and the lure of future glory, but few can, like Jack Arkwright, have signed for a motorbike! While playing for the strangely-titled Sutton Comics, an amateur side in St Helens, Jack was approached by the town's professional club to sign terms but, having had trials as a goalkeeper with Liverpool, he was not too keen to throw in his lot with the Rugby League code. Until, that is, he saw the first all-electric battery lamps on a gleaming motorbike in a St Helens shop window.

'The bike cost £72.00 and I wanted it badly', he remembers. 'With my £50.00 signing-on fee, my first match payment and a few pounds I got for having trials I was able to buy it.' And what a controversial and exciting career that motorbike launched for this giant of a forward, $16\frac{1}{2}$ stones and 6 feet 3 inches tall.

Jack played for St Helens (1929–34) and Warrington (1934–39) in an era when the forwards had to be big, powerful men to withstand all the scrummages – there were often as many as 60 per match on average. For their £4.00 match-winning pay ('£1.00 extra because I was an international') they had to spar up to each other in the middle of the field and tackle, tackle and tackle again. Rarely running great distances with the ball, they needed to be more adept at the 'dribble', especially popular with Yorkshire forwards. This involved dropping the ball at their feet and working their way up field rather in the manner of a soccer player dribbling the ball at his feet. Rugby League forward play was extremely physical in those days with no quarter asked or given, even among one's own team-mates. Indeed, on the boat to Australia prior to Jack's controversial tour in 1936, the British forwards organised boxing matches among themselves throughout the seven-week voyage. No wonder Jack Arkwright's punches got him into so much trouble Down Under!

The exchanges between the forwards in that 1936 Test series were fierce, Jack Arkwright being sent off in the third Test at Sydney by referee Lal Deane. Ray Stehr, the fiery Australian forward, later followed him but, unlike Jack, as he left the field he didn't suffer the accompanying strains of the brass band playing *Goodnight Sweetheart*. Nor did Jack's long walks finish at the Sydney Cricket Ground, for in a country game he achieved the dubious distinction of becoming the only player ever to be sent from the field twice in the same match: 'I tackled a player a little hard and another player raced across to argue with me over the tackle', he explains. 'I thumped him and, although I was sent off by the referee, their captain persuaded him to bring me back again. I think they wanted to take their revenge on me but when I thumped their captain, Kingston, I was finally dismissed for the second time in the match.'

Jack Arkwright keeps his eye firmly on the ball during Great Britain's Test match against Australia in 1936.

Such incidents should not detract from Jack's ability as a forward, and his six caps for Great Britain when with Warrington are testimony to his hard tackling and strong running. In an age when forwards were hardly noted for their tryscoring ability Jack's six tries in ten appearances on that 1936 tour indicate what a fine eye he had for support play.

ERIC ASHTON

b. 24.1.1935
Wigan, Great Britain

Whenever one mentions the Wigan and Great Britain centre, Eric Ashton, the name of Billy Boston, his wing partner, immediately springs to mind and images of the duo's feats down the touchline colour the memory. And yet I can exclusively reveal that Boston was not Eric Ashton's first wing partner – I was! At the age of 11 we played together in our local Congregational Church field in St Helens. He was a stylish player even then, when 40 or 50 of us used to play Rugby League all day long in the summer holidays.

'Stylish' is the word I would use to describe the play of this lean, 6 feet 2-inch centre for, despite his undoubted scoring ability with Wigan (231 tries and 448 goals), it was essentially his leadership and his playmaking for others that made an impact on a game. That Eric captained Wigan to six Wembley Challenge Cup finals between 1958 and 1966 and led Great Britain to victory in the 1960 World Cup and to an Ashes triumph on the 1962 tour Down Under speaks volumes for his uncanny ability to get the best out of his team-mates. Using a quiet, constructive word and rarely raising his voice to the players, he commanded a respect on the field afforded to few players by professionals ever jealous of their own abilities. He led from the front and most of his time was spent in creating opportunities for others, such was his tactical awareness during a match.

In the modern game of Rugby League, in Britain especially, there has been a dearth of creative centres who make play for their wingmen, a characteristic considered the priority of any centre in the 1940s and '50s. Eric Ashton proved to be as adept at scoring at international level as his modern counterpart, Garry Schofield, registering the prolific total of 51 tries on his 1958 and 1962 Lions tours to Australasia, but as a creator of play he has had few peers in modern times. Eric's long stride and deceptive pace fooled many a defender who gave him too much room on the outside and his outrageous dummy has seen many a would-be tackler miss his man.

But it is his partnership with Billy Boston for which I best remember him. That partnership began in 1956 when, although a St Helens lad, he joined Wigan for £150, striking terror into all opponents, and severely embarrassing a few, including me! His scissors move with Billy Boston was perfected to a fine art and, whether he was retaining the ball himself or passing inside to the thundering Billy, it was a ploy which split open many a defence, and a few other things as well, as I can vouch! In one Good Friday Derby match in the early 1960s between my own club, St Helens, and Wigan I had devised a defensive strategy with my loose forward colleague, Bill Major, to cope with Eric's scissors movement. We practised our move from the scrum, but to no avail. Eric Ashton raced out towards the touchline, Billy Boston roared inside with the ball

Although renowned for his creative centre play, Eric Ashton was a prolific tryscorer in his own right for Wigan.

in a move so well executed that I tackled my own team-mate, Bill Major, with such force that he was led from the field to have stitches inserted into his cut eyebrow. Needless to say Boston scored a try beneath the posts.

Such tactical ability and powers of leadership were naturally to lead Eric into becoming the player-coach at Wigan from 1963 to 1969 and, once his playing days were over, he continued as coach until 1973 when he moved a few miles to take charge of local rivals St Helens. He was an outstanding thinker on the game, and brought such dignity to his sport that he was awarded the M.B.E. in June 1966.

PUIG AUBERT

One of the most vivid impressions of my youth is the sight of the old rickety wooden fence which used to surround Knowsley Road, St Helens' playing pitch, in the immediate post-War years. I can still see the small, round, tubby shape of French full back Puig Aubert leaning against the fencing, chatting to the spectators while his team launched a furious attack at the other end of the field. Such was his apparent nonchalance towards the activities of his team-mates, that he even smoked a cigarette, kindly offered by a spectator. Yet Puig Aubert, or Aubert Puig as he should really be known – his surname is so common in the South of France that he reversed his name for easier identification – was to emerge as one of the greatest full backs of any nation and certainly the greatest influence on *rugby à treize* in France since the Second World War.

b. 24.3.1925
Carcassonne, Celtic de Paris, France

Puig Aubert – an inspirational French captain Down Under in 1951.

In a playing career which spanned the years 1944–57 Puig Aubert displayed an uncanny timing of a pass, an incisive sidestep, a gift for fluent handling and, above all, a penchant for kicking goals. Although he was troubled at the latter end of his career by an ever-increasing weight problem, which resulted in a loss of mobility about the pitch, he never lost the handling and kicking ability for which he is so renowned.

'Pipette', as he was affectionately known by his supporters, on account of his habit of having a smoke on the field, had safe hands to cope with all types of weather conditions. The night before Carcassonne's historic 11–8 win over Wigan in March 1947 heavy snow had fallen for several hours, and the game itself was played during a blinding snowstorm, yet 'Pipette' took great delight in fielding the ball with one hand whenever the Wigan players put any high kicks upfield. Ever a showman, he was responsible for thrusting France to the centre stage of the Rugby League world in a very different climate in Australia in 1951, a year for which he will always be remembered.

Serious doubts about the strength of the French team and the futility of France embarking on a trip to Australia in the summer of 1951 seemed to be confirmed by the poor results in the country games on the tour. Sensationally, however, France, led by Puig Aubert, won the first Test 26–15 and the Australian public were fired by the brilliant attacking football of the supposed 'no hopers'. The Test series proved to be one of the most spectacular in the history of Test rugby, France winning the third and deciding Test 35–14 before a crowd of 67,009 appreciative Australians. And Puig Aubert was France's hero. His total of 163 points on the tour broke all existing points records, while his record of 18 goals from 18 attempts in the three Test matches stands today. Deadly accurate with his boot, whether kicking goals or setting up his favourite ploy, the drop goal, his total of 46 international caps bears testimony to the skills of France's most exciting full back.

HARRY BATH

Both as a youngster and later as a player, I was haunted by the name of Harry Bath. As I leaned over the wooden perimeter fencing at the St Helens ground in the late 1940s, the sight of Harry Bath, Warrington's powerful second row or prop forward, charging down the pitch sent shudders through my tiny frame. And 20 years later, when I had the honour of representing Great Britain in the 1968 World Cup, it was Harry Bath who, as coach to the Australian team, masterminded their victory and a 25–10 win over my team at the Sydney Cricket Ground. Whether playing or coaching, he was one of the leading personalities in Rugby League although, sadly for Australian fans, they saw little of him when in his prime.

After a short playing career for Queensland in 1945, followed by an even briefer stay with the Balmain club in Sydney, Harry Bath signed for Barrow in Cumbria for the sum of £1,000. Unfortunately for Barrow he could not settle and, for a further fee of £1,500, he moved further south to Warrington in 1947. He was to be the cornerstone of Warrington's success in the post-War years and, as captain and player, he

b. 28.11.1924
Balmain, Barrow,
Warrington, St George

A typical forceful run by Warrington's Australian prop Harry Bath results in a try.

was to play a huge part in their two Challenge Cup wins of 1950 and 1954 and their Championship win in 1955 against the mighty Oldham. Harry was to become, in 1950, the first overseas player to captain a winning side at Wembley when he helped the Wires defeat local rivals Widnes 19–0.

His two goals in the Championship final of 1955 proved to be the vital difference when both sides were locked in battle at 3–3 (a try was worth only three points at that time). Indeed, such was Harry's goalkicking prowess that he topped the British goalkicking charts in 1952–53 with 170 goals and the following year with 153 goals. Even later in life his uncanny accuracy did not desert him – he once kicked eight goals in one match for St George, Sydney in 1957 and amassed 108 goals in the 1958 season.

The migration of quality players from Australia immediately after the 1939–45 War meant that many like Harry Bath and Huddersfield's Johnny Hunter never gained the honour of wearing the green and gold jersey. The 'Other Nationalities' side was the only substitute available to them for their lack of international recognition, and for this team Harry and his fellow countryman Arthur Clues formed a fiery second row partnership.

Although he was a big man, weighing well over 15 stones at his peak, Harry had a surprising turn of speed and could prove devastating if allowed to get into his stride. Like most Australian forwards, he was naturally tough and a hard tackler but over his ten seasons' play at Wilderspool with Warrington he developed the art of a skilled ball player, a craft much envied by Australian forwards. The British style of play has always encouraged a forward to develop the technique of slipping the ball out of the tackles and to be able to open out play with an array of passes. When Harry returned Down Under in 1957 the St George club were shrewd enough to realise his talents and, with Harry as the pivot of their midfield play, both he and they enjoyed three excellent seasons. In the few seasons he spent with St George the Australian fans appreciated just why the name of Harry Bath is held in such awe in Britain. And, later, when he coached their Grand Final winning sides of 1977 and 1979 against Parramatta and Canterbury Barkstown, they came to realise just what rugby knowledge and tactical expertise he had learned during the harsh northern winters in England.

BILLY BATTEN

When Billy Batten joined Hull from Hunslet in April 1913, he was paid £14.00 per match, with a larger bonus for Cup matches. When one considers that my average match payment for St Helens 50 years later was only £20.00 for a win, it is clear just how important he was to the fortunes of the Humberside club.

His ability and standing within the League code at the beginning of the First World War is further illustrated by the fact that his transfer fee between the two clubs was fixed at £600. That figure, for the only time in history, doubled the previous record fee of £300 paid by Oldham to Salford for Jim Lomas, Batten's captain on the first ever tour of Australia in 1910. Billy Batten, a big, black-haired centre and occasional wing, was indeed recognised as one of the outstanding personalities in the early years of the Rugby League or, as it was known until 1922, the Northern Rugby Football Union.

Born in the tiny mining village of Kinsley, near Fitzwilliam in Yorkshire, Billy Batten was one of the early pioneers of Test rugby, starring first for the Hunslet club prior to his transfer to Hull in 1913. Billy played in eight Tests against Australia in an incredibly long span of Test rugby between 1908 and 1921, and achieved the proud distinction of playing in all three of the Tests in the first ever series between Great Britain (or England as they were then known) and Australia in season 1908–09. Although Billy scored two tries in that first Test on 12th December 1908 at Park Royal, London, the home of Queen's Park Rangers soccer club, and helped his team to draw 22–22, the game of Rugby League is especially indebted to him and to his colleagues for taking the first steps to popularise the League code on a national basis. By playing Test matches outside the heartlands of League at Newcastle, Birmingham and London these early pioneers sowed the first seeds of national expansion, even if the seeds failed to take root effectively until the 1980s when the likes of Fulham, Mansfield and Carlisle were welcomed into the fold.

During his 11-year stay at Hull, before he moved for a very short period to Wakefield Trinity, he helped his team to win every trophy available, and for his feats he was further well rewarded with the first ever £1,000 testimonial benefit. He became the idol of Yorkshire and was appreciated at both Hunslet and Hull for his ability to score tries by powering his huge bulk directly at would-be tacklers, rather in the style of a Sherman tank. Never veering, he would run through opponents but, occasionally, and much to the delight of the fans, he used more unorthodox methods of beating a man.

Billy is credited as the first player to introduce one tactic into Rugby League which, although it brought gasps from the crowds, had to be banned on account of the incidence of dangerous accidents. When

b. 26.5.1889
Hunslet, Hull, Wakefield Trinity, Great Britain

*When Billy Batten moved to
Hull in 1913 he became the
highest paid player in the
League at £14.00 per match.*

playing on the wing he would build up speed as he ran towards his
opponent and then suddenly leap over his head to the roars of the crowd.
However, one day when he attempted this, a famous New Zealand player
by the name of Opai Asher is reputed to have leaped into the air at the
same time in an attempt to topple Batten. A fearsome and spectacular
sight it may have been, but, thankfully, for safety reasons it is no longer
permissible in the game.

ARTIE BEETSON

Whenever I watch the antics of two heavyweight boxing champions before the opening round, listening to the referee's instructions in the centre of the ring and staring eyeball to eyeball at each other I am reminded of my first confrontation with big, 6 feet 2-inch and 16½-stone Australian Test prop Artie Beetson. Prior to the opening match of the 1968 World Cup tournament in Australia and New Zealand we stood and stared at each other on the famous Sydney Cricket Ground. The National Anthems were playing but I confess that the strains of *God Save The Queen* were lost on me as I weighed up my adversary for that afternoon. And he took some weighing up, for he was a huge man and a fearsome opponent on the rugby field. He was tough, occasionally rough – he was one of only 15 Australians dismissed from the field in the history of Anglo/Australian Test matches – and yet he was one of the cleverest prop forwards ever to wear the green and gold jersey of Australia.

Artie Beetson gained ten caps in Anglo/Australian Test matches as a prop or second row forward, mostly due to his uncompromising play in the pack. But he was also awarded those caps because he was one of the best ball-handlers produced Down Under. Artie, in the British manner of Brian McTigue or Brian Edgar, had the ability to slip the pass out of the tackle to a colleague racing up in support. He had the size and strength to stand upright in the tackle, attract two or three defenders around him and then still be able to continue the movement with one of his deft one-handed passes. Such forwards are invaluable to a pack and it is significant that for eight seasons between 1966 and 1974 he was rarely out of the Australian Test side.

It is hard to imagine that this giant of a forward, often troubled by weight problems at the latter end of his career, started as a centre with the Redcliffe club in Brisbane where he learned his handling skills. Those skills were enjoyed by the Balmain club from 1966 until 1970, when he had a one-season spell with Hull Kingston Rovers in England before joining Eastern Suburbs in 1971. His ability to think constructively and tactically on the game is best shown by his commitment to coaching, first as captain and player-coach with the 'Roosters' in 1977 and later as coach to Parramatta, Redcliffe and to his former club Eastern Suburbs in the 1980s.

Like Jack Arkwright and Ray Stehr, whose fiery antics on the field raised the emotions of the crowds watching the 1936 Ashes series, Artie Beetson's involvement in clashes with Syd Hynes and Cliff Watson in the 1970 Test series aroused the passions of the public. Whatever misgivings we might have over tough play in sport, the characters who indulge in the odd bout of it are often loved by the crowds, their names and their deeds frequently becoming part of the legendary folklore of

b. 21.1.1945
Redcliffe, Balmain, Hull
Kingston Rovers, Eastern
Suburbs, Australia

Great Britain v Australia, 1973. Artie Beetson draws the Great Britain tacklers before he prepares to pass the ball.

the game. Artie Beetson is no exception, for even the British supporters still talk of his ferocious clashes with his opposite prop, the Lions' Cliff Watson, in that 1970 series which resulted in him being dismissed from the field in the deciding third Test for the Ashes. His clash with the equally fiery Lions centre Syd Hynes in the second Test of that series resulted in Hynes also leaving the field for an early bath. Yes, Artie Beetson was the stuff of which legends are made.

DEAN BELL

In Rugby League there is no substitute for speed. Many a player who has paraded all the skills necessary to play in the backs at the highest level has often been found wanting in that final yard to the tryline. Many a centre has failed to advance his cause because he lacks speed off the mark or a sustained burst over 30 or 40 yards to break the cover and race clear of defenders. Not so with Wigan's Kiwi international, Dean Bell, whose blistering pace and full repertoire of centre skills have been a key factor in bringing all five major trophies in the British league to Wigan between 1986 and 1988.

b. 29.4.1962
Manakau, Carlisle, Leeds,
Eastern Suburbs, Wigan,
New Zealand

Wigan's Kiwi international Dean Bell makes a characteristic burst through the centre.

A New Zealand Test player since 1983, it would be appropriate to label Dean Bell as an international player in every sense of the word. When the Rugby League's International Board relaxed their ban on overseas signings in 1983 Dean was one of the first to take advantage of the new independence for players and to move away from the traditional status of part-time professionalism. In the early days of the breakaway from Rugby Union in 1895 the ruling League authorities insisted that a man must be in full-time normal employment before being eligible to play for his League club at the weekend. So strictly was this law adhered to that part-time jobs like bookmakers' runners or snooker cue markers were also banned. Hence the idea of part-time Rugby League was enshrined in the traditions of the sport. The new freedom of players to roam the world, as well as the enhanced prestige and financial standing of Rugby League, has enabled players to become full-time professionals, earning considerable salaries playing in both hemispheres during the winter and summer.

Between 1982 and 1988 Dean's travels led him from his Manakau club in New Zealand to England where he played for Carlisle and Leeds before joining Wigan. During the English summers he joined Eastern Suburbs in Sydney, where he played with considerable success. Such travelling around the world and such contact with the best players of all nations has obviously helped to make Dean the complete player that he is today.

His selection on the wing to mark the Australian flyer, Kerry Boustead, in his first Test match in 1983 showed his speed, and this was never better highlighted than when he finished off a movement with a try in the Challenge Cup final of 1988 for Wigan against Halifax. Although small in stature, Dean is a very powerful runner and an exceptionally keen tackler, able to stop the flow of an opposition threequarter line by moving in quickly from the centre position to stop the stand off. His attitude and self-discipline off the field, developed in Australia when with Eastern Suburbs, are exemplary and have further enhanced his career.

GILBERT BENAUSSE

Having made the move from Rugby Union to Rugby League barely six months previously and eager to learn as much about my new code as I could, I watched the Test match between Great Britain and France at Wigan in February 1962. I learned little about forward play, but how grateful I was to see a classic display from the French stand off Gilbert Benausse, whose two tries and four goals (a record points haul for a French player in Anglo/French Tests) spurred his side to their first win on British soil. Benausse that day was not only constructive and creative

b. 21.1.1932
Carcassonne, Toulouse,
Lezignam, France

Gilbert Benausse carries the ball loosely, away from his body, ever looking to pass.

but proved an opportunist and a clever support player in amassing his points. A feature of his play was a technique which, sadly, we see too little of in the modern game – the smother tackle. Hard-tackling threequarters like Billy Boston (Wigan), Alan Davies (Wigan and Oldham) and Duggie Greenall (St Helens) perfected the art of moving in quickly on an attacker and, with an upright tackle, covering the player's body with their chest and arms to stop the player from passing the ball. Benausse was a master in this department.

From the age of 17, when he joined Carcassonne, throughout his two World Cup tournaments in 1954 and 1957 and France's successful tour of Australia in 1955, he was an accurate goalkicker with a long, powerful kick. Sadly for Gilbert, despite the eight goals and one try that made him the leading points-scorer in the 1957 World Cup, he had few opportunities to kick goals in his 49 internationals on account of the even greater talents of his team-mate at both club and international level, Puig Aubert.

Gilbert Benausse developed his game in the golden age of French rugby, the 1950s, when his skills were fashioned by the ability and experience of those great players alongside him. Established stars like Raymond Contrastin and Jacques Merquey helped him to mature into the most skilful of midfield backs, moving one contemporary writer to say: 'Benausse, when carrying the ball, is a delight to see: three or four yards away he will dummy his opponent. He will poise on one foot, then the other, perhaps hesitate, and with a quick change of direction he is past, leaving his opponent clutching nothing but grass and fresh air'.

BRIAN BEVAN

Never judge a player on first impressions. Leeds did, and lost the services of the greatest winger ever to grace the game of Rugby League. When Brian Bevan, a stoker in the Australian Navy was in Portsmouth in 1945, awaiting a refit for his ship *H.M.A.S. Australia*, he contacted Bill Shankland, a golf professional, to try to arrange a trial with the famous Yorkshire club. Unfortunately, despite his brown tan, his 11-stone, wiry frame and knobbly knees did not appeal to the Leeds committee, who advised him to try elsewhere. Thankfully for Rugby League he did and, having played his first match for Warrington in November 1945, he went on to score 796 tries, a world career best, before retiring from Blackpool Borough in February 1964. One could hardly blame the first instincts of those Leeds committeemen and yet the thin, balding figure, usually swathed in knee and elbow bandages, camouflaged a talent for scoring tries that will probably never be equalled.

Brian came from a rugby-mad Sydney family; his father played for Eastern Suburbs, and he played rugby as a youngster on Bondi Beach and at the Randwick High School. Shame on the school that, when I visited it with my own school rugby team in 1981, no one at the establishment realised that Brian Bevan was one of their most famous sporting sons. Like most Sydney youngsters he was taken to the big League matches at the Cricket Ground by his father, and, on his way home, he would sidestep all the telegraph poles on his route. Here was the beginning of one of his most notable assets: his ability to sidestep off both feet.

Brian represented the 'Other Nationalities', a team which was very popular in international competition in the 1940s and '50s, on 26 occasions but never played rugby in his native land. Thus he must remain the greatest winger never to play for Australia. In his 16 seasons with Warrington his uncanny ability to score tries rarely eluded him; indeed, it allowed him to gain over 740 tries for the Cheshire club, scoring seven tries on two occasions, six tries on four occasions and record a hat trick 69 times. Quite incredible! And he could kick goals too, when called upon, as his 35 goals in his first season with the Wires illustrates.

Brian had the first priority of any winger, sheer speed, and such was his prowess in this department that in the company of Stan McCormick, Griff Jenkins and others, immediately after the Second World War, he raced at many professional sprint handicap meetings, rarely being beaten. A sidestep, a body swerve, instant acceleration and an instinctive footballer's brain were among his other attributes but essentially he was an unorthodox winger, often scoring from unbelievable positions on the field. He had a masterly timing of the interception and knew when to cross-kick the ball – he would often time his run to arrive at the precise

b. 24.6.1924
Warrington, Blackpool
Borough

moment of the bounce of the ball, thus allowing him to regain possession without decreasing his speed. He had, as Steve Llewellyn (a fine Welsh wing with St Helens) describes, an uncanny ability to evade an opponent by stopping dead in full flight: 'Brian would stop dead, anchors down, forcing the full back to race past him'.

Beneath all the unique skills mentioned, I witnessed at first hand the sheer dedication, professionalism and the competitive instincts which kept him at the top for so long. When invited to take part in a knockabout exhibition match between two teams of retired players at the St Helens ground in the mid-1970s I arrived early at the ground, the first as I thought. Not so, for although all of the players, now well past their prime, were treating the match as little more than an exhibition romp there was one player already on the masseur's table, being rubbed down and having bandages applied – Brian Bevan. Although in his 50s he was as eager as ever to perform his repertoire of skills. And he did: he scored two tries with his characteristic runs down the wing while the rest of us, in spite of our relative youth, gasped for breath in midfield.

OPPOSITE: *Brian Bevan, widely considered to be the greatest wingman of all time, cannot evade the attentions of the touch judge on one of his dashes down the wing.*

TOMMY BISHOP

b. 15.10.1940
Blackpool Borough, Barrow,
St Helens, Cronulla,
Illawarra, Great Britain

When you weigh $10\frac{1}{2}$ stones and stand barely 5 feet 4 inches tall you have to be cheeky to list basketball as one of your hobbies in a Test match programme. At that height and weight you need more than cheek to compete in the tough world of international Rugby League where the occasional 16-stone forward is lurking, ever ready to pounce on the unsuspecting back. Tommy Bishop, my contemporary in the 1960s at St Helens, had all the qualities needed to succeed and the ambition to overcome the limitations of his physical frame.

Tommy made his first entry into professional rugby with Blackpool Borough, having signed from the amateur ranks in 1959, and then spent some time at Barrow before making the vital move to St Helens in 1966. This move was the key to St Helens' capture of four cups that season: the Championship Trophy, the League Leaders Trophy, the Challenge Cup and the Lancashire League Cup.

I well remember his first match for the club which revealed all the qualities that made him such a fine player. Having lost to Wakefield Trinity in a league match, Saints were drawn to play again at Wakefield on the following Saturday in the Challenge Cup. Our journey over the Pennines was a tortuous one, there being a heavy carpet of snow lying everywhere, and on arrival at the Belle Vue ground we were greeted by a muddy heap which passed for a pitch. The snow had been swept to the surrounding barriers, mud and water were everywhere, and the morale of the team was low. But new boy Tommy Bishop revived everyone with his infectious enthusiasm, scored a try beneath the posts and chivvied the team to its best display of the season.

Not blessed with size or great speed, Tommy was a battler who never gave up and was at his best when the odds were stacked against him. He possessed no sidestep but fooled many an opponent with a deceptive shimmy of the body. But above all he had a shrewd footballing brain which allowed him to serve up an endless array of defence-splitting passes and touch-finding kicks. His tackling, for one so small, had to be seen to be believed. He snapped at the big forwards in the ferocious manner of a terrier snapping at the heels of a postman.

In the 1966–67 Test series against Australia his half back partnerships with Alan Hardisty or Roger Millward proved troublesome to the Kangaroos and his form on the Great Britain World Cup trip to Australia and New Zealand in 1968 was such that the rich clubs of Sydney were anxious to sign this little dynamo. Cronulla, one of the unfashionable Sydney clubs, finally captured Tommy as captain-coach in season 1969–70, and alongside another of his ex-Saints colleagues, Cliff Watson, he unexpectedly took Cronulla to the Sydney Grand Final in 1973, only to lose 10–7 to the more glamorous Manly club. Brisbane, Illawarra and North Sydney later called upon his services as a player or coach before the 'Little General' finally called it a day.

Scrum halves, by the very nature of their position close to the big forwards, are usually tough, gritty, uncompromising and at times arrogant. Tommy Bishop had all those qualities in abundance. It must be especially gratifying for him to see his son Paul playing in the finest of the Bishop traditions with Warrington and Cronulla.

OPPOSITE: *Tommy Bishop, Great Britain's fiery scrum half, escapes the clutches of Australia's John Wittenberg in the third Test in 1966 at the Sydney Cricket Ground.*

BILLY BOSTON

b. 6.8.1934
Wigan, Blackpool Borough,
Great Britain

On many a cold, damp, wintry morning I still wake experiencing soreness and pain in my shoulder joints, not from any arthritic or rheumatic condition, but from countless tackles attempted (and I stress 'attempted') on Wigan's barnstorming, blockbusting wing of the 1950s and '60s, William John Boston or 'Billy B'. The sight of this thundering 15-stone powerhouse hurtling down the right for yet another of the 571 tries scored in his career was often enough to scare the most dedicated of cover tacklers. If you made contact with the swivel of his hip or the force of his thighs you were often left with a lasting memory firmly imprinted in your flesh. Billy Boston was quite possibly, along with his fellow ex-Cardiff Rugby Union player, Jim Sullivan, the most famous player ever to don the cherry and white hooped jersey of the great Lancashire club.

Billy was a sensation even in his younger days as an 18-year-old youth, weighing 12 stones 8 pounds, when he played Rugby Union for the Welsh Boys Club and later for Cardiff Internationals Athletic Club. When he registered for national service in the Army at the Royal Corps of Signals at Catterick in 1952 his feats soon attracted the attention of every Rugby League talent scout in the country. Playing in a team of combined talents in those civilised days when League and Union stars played together in the Armed Services competitions, Billy Boston illustrated all the skills that were to stamp him as a future Rugby League star. Although Phil Jackson, the Barrow and Great Britain League centre, and Reg Higgins and Phil Horrocks-Taylor, two England Union internationals, featured in that star-studded army divisional side, Boston was the player they all came to see.

Despite scoring over 126 tries for the Royal Signals in one season as an 18-year-old and being described by Pat Marshall, the highly-respected *Daily Express* Union correspondent as 'quite simply one of the greatest running backs I have ever seen', it was Rugby League and, strangely, not Welsh Rugby Union which appreciated his talents. Although he signed for Wigan on 13th March 1953 for a sum of £3,000, it was some months before he played his first match for the club, his signing having been kept a secret to allow him to complete his service rugby commitments. But it was not long after his first match, against Barrow's 'A' team in October, that he was on his way with the Great Britain touring team to Australia in the summer of 1954 after playing barely a handful of games for Wigan. And what a momentous tour he had!

Gaining the first of his 31 Great Britain international caps in the second Test against Australia on that 1954 tour, he went on to break the existing tour tryscoring record with 36 tries and to equal the record for the number of tries scored in a Test match by grabbing four tries

OPPOSITE: *Billy Boston powers around a despairing Workington Town tackler.*

30

against New Zealand in Auckland. A further Lions tour in 1962 and participation in two World Cup tournaments in 1957 and 1960 added to the glittering international career of a player who scarcely had a weakness.

In his early playing days in the 1950s Billy weighed around 13 stones and allied tremendous pace to his other undoubted skills. By the 1960s his weight had increased to 15 stones and his still surprising speed made him all the more difficult to stop. He cultivated a short, neat sidestep, developed an outside swerve and used a hand-off like the kick of a mule. He could run round you or through you depending on his inclination. Yet he was also, when needed, the complete footballer.

Having started his career as a full back in his Union days Billy Boston was called upon many times by Wigan to take the field in the centre or stand off positions, occasionally even in the forwards, but always he displayed a keen tactical appreciation and showed an ability to create movements for others. His body-jarring tackles often bordered on the horrific. Billy had the ability, so rarely seen in the modern game, to rush in from his wing position and take out the opposition centre with an all-enveloping body tackle before the centre could pass the ball to his wing partner. Many an attacking movement down the Wigan right wing has been stopped in its infancy by his precision timing of the tackle.

Billy, now mine host at 'The Griffin' hotel, barely 100 yards away from Central Park, Wigan, where he is still adored by the faithful fans, played 11 matches for Blackpool Borough at the latter end of his career between 1969 and 1971. But always he will be remembered for his deeds in the Wigan No. 2 jersey which he wore with such pride in six Wembley Challenge Cup finals.

LES BOYD

b. 17.11.1956
Western Suburbs, Manly,
Warrington, Australia

Rugby League can be very punishing on the bodies of its players who have to endure so many bone-crunching tackles. Obviously, in a game which demands such physical confrontation among its players the highest priority must be placed on discipline and the difference between hard, uncompromising play and foul play is often very slight. Some players, such as Les Boyd, tread a narrow line in their approach to foul play. This Australian Test forward's all-action play and wholehearted approach to tackling often led him into trouble with referees and, ultimately, the Australian Board of Control. Yet, although I would never condone some of Les's actions, many of which cost him months of suspension from the game, I have always been a great admirer of his committed approach to rugby.

During his 12 months' suspension in 1984 for breaking the jaw of Darryl Brahman, the Queensland forward, I happened to come across Les working hard in a Sydney gymnasium. I have never seen a greater determination to come back from obscurity or a player so eager to prove himself again. And this he did when he joined Warrington in 1985, rewarding the club's gamble with three seasons of outstanding play. Although he was plagued with a succession of breaks to his arms at the latter end of his career, Les Boyd led the Wires to the Premiership final where they emerged as 38–10 winners over Halifax in 1986 and he collected the Harry Sunderland Trophy for Man of the Match. In that game Les's two tries revealed his fine turn of speed for a large, 16-stone forward; his scrummaging, in conjunction with that of Kiwi Test prop Kevin Tamati, resulted in a monopoly of possession. He is one of the few Rugby League forwards of recent times who has concentrated on the art of scrummaging. A tribute to Les Boyd's display that day labelled his efforts as a show of 'controlled aggression and inspiring leadership'. How well the words captured his playing style.

As a youngster with the Cootamundra club in southern New South Wales, surprisingly as a centre, Les showed such promise that he was selected to represent the famous Australian schools side which went through Europe undefeated in 1972. And it was obvious that, barring serious injury, a full Test career was just around the corner. That Test career, which brought him over 19 international caps, saw him undertake two tours of Great Britain with the Kangaroos in 1978 and 1982, first as a Western Suburbs player and then as a representative of Manly-Warringah. His form as a prop forward on the 1982 'Invincibles' tour, in which he represented Australia in all five Tests against Great Britain and France, was staggering. He proved a fearsome competitor and helped the Kangaroos establish a dominance up front through their fitness and technique that was never to be questioned by any club or national side. Few players, either, questioned Les Boyd's dominance over them on that tour as he scattered numerous defences with his short 30-yard bursts or his crunching tackles. Mostly within the laws, I would add!

Tough prop Les Boyd touches down in Warrington's 38–10 Premiership Trophy victory over Halifax.

STANLEY BROGDEN

Whatever skills a back in Rugby League may possess, whether they be handling, passing, a sidestep or a swerve, there is no denying that the most useful attribute is speed. Pure speed can take a player beyond the reach of the most ferocious tackler, can extricate him from the tightest of corners and can provide the final element in a tryscoring movement. And, among his other qualities, it was the pace and balanced running of Stan Brogden which elevated him above his contemporaries and made him one of the most gifted threequarters of the 1930s.

Stan, a talented soccer player, inherited his aptitude for rugby from his father, who was a keen follower of the game and who was delighted to see his son make his debut for Bradford Northern in 1927. His stay at Odsal was short, and his career is best known for his exploits with Huddersfield, whom he joined in 1929, and Leeds, following his signing for the club in the 1933–34 season at a world-record fee of £1,200. That fee was indicative of Brogden's ability, especially his penchant for scoring or creating tries at Test level.

During an international career in which he gained 16 Test caps, 11 of which were awarded for his appearances against Australia in five Test series between 1930 and 1937, his record in his first outings against the Kangaroos in 1932 best illustrates his particular skills. Sheer speed, which enabled him to outpace all of his opponents, was Stanley Brogden's main weapon in his rugby armoury and it was his try in the third Test against Australia which proved decisive in winning the Ashes for Great Britain. His ability to race onto a pass at top speed, shoot through a gap and cover the remaining 25 yards without the opposition laying a finger on him helped his side to snatch an 18–13 victory. But he had a rugby brain as well and was never afraid to kick the ball when the need arose. A try by big Castleford centre Arthur Atkinson in the first Test of that 1932 series was created by Brogden's accurate kick to the right wing where Alf Ellaby had the easiest of takes to hand on the ball for Atkinson to score. Such was his pace and outside swerve that he was able to play on the wing in the 1936 Anglo/Australian series. The hard, dry grounds of Australia proved ideal conditions for such an athlete. He was also well suited to the game of sevens, which he played with finesse in the competitions at Huddersfield and Leeds in the mid-1930s.

Jack Arkwright, his colleague on that tour Down Under in 1936, tells the story of how he started a sprint race between Brogden and a cheeky Australian who had made sarcastic remarks calling into question Stan's speed. The prize was to be the Australian's binoculars, valued at £2.00 which was no mean sum in those days. Stan Brogden informed Jack that he would let the Aussie retain the lead for the first 90 yards to maintain the onlookers' interest. This he did, claiming the binoculars with a blistering spurt in the final ten yards.

b. 15.3.1910
Bradford Northern,
Huddersfield, Leeds, Hull,
Rochdale, Salford, Great
Britain

One of the most gifted threequarters of the 1930s, Stan Brogden, shows his pace as he chases after a kick ahead.

JIM BROUGH

b. 5.11.1903
Leeds, Great Britain

Unlike most great players, Jim Brough did not learn his trade as a youngster kicking an oval ball around a park pitch or passing a rolled-up newspaper in a game of touch rugby with his pals. Surprisingly, for one blessed with such a tactical rugby brain, he never touched an oval ball until he was 17 years old, but when he did, for Silloth and Cumbria Rugby Union teams, he quickly made up for lost time. By season 1924–25 he had represented England at Rugby Union against the All Blacks, pitting his wits against New Zealand's greatest full back, George Nepia, himself a Rugby League player much later with Streatham and Mitcham in London. It was obvious that his attacking style of play would attract the League scouts but Jim Brough, as he explains, was unwilling to sign professional forms before gaining his second Union cap against Wales: 'All I had in my pocket was a shilling and a return ticket between Silloth and Carlisle where I was to meet Mr Sam Jones, the Swinton secretary. He placed £350 in notes on the table, but I wanted to play against Wales'.

That he eventually signed for Leeds in June 1925 was perhaps inevitable, but it was by no means the formality many expected, for Jim's services were much in demand by Liverpool Football Club. They wanted him to understudy their famous England goalkeeper, Elisha Scott. But, as Jim Brough honestly admitted, the financial considerations influenced his decision: 'Liverpool scouts watched me play at full back in the Cheshire v Cumbria Rugby Union match at Birkenhead but, if I had signed for soccer, under the Football Association's rules I was only entitled to a signing on fee of £10.00. I was paid almost £1,000 in cash by Leeds to play Rugby League'. They got a bargain, though, for Jim Brough represented them in over 442 matches.

He was unfortunate in that his career coincided with that of the peerless Jim Sullivan at Wigan who, as a full back, restricted Brough's international appearances. Jim Brough nonetheless quickly established himself at Test level, making his debut for Great Britain as a centre in the first Test against Australia in Brisbane on the 1928 tour. He went on to captain the 1936 tour when Jim Sullivan declined to make his fourth trip due to his wife's illness.

It was his rivalry with Jim Sullivan for which this fine, unorthodox attacking player is best remembered. Sullivan was without equal as a goalkicker, yet Jim Brough always treasured the trophy he won in a world goalkicking competition held at Toowoomba during the 1928 tour – especially as the donor of the trophy had been so confident of Sullivan's victory that he had had the Wigan full back's name inscribed on the trophy before the competition started!

His touch-finding duels with Sullivan are legendary and reflect a phase of the game that was a delight to watch in the pre-Second World

War days. Following a tackle, when the ball was dropped by the tackled player from waist height at the play the ball, any player could attempt to retrieve the ball for their side. Hence, under the rule then operating, it was dangerous to be caught in possession near the try line if a team was not certain, as it would be today under the six tackle rule, of retaining possession. The result was absorbing, long-kicking duels between the two full backs, each seeking to find touch near their opponents' line or to pressure their opponent into a mistake. Brough for Leeds and Sullivan of Wigan were the two artists in this tactical warfare, each sending the ball 70 yards downfield and making the other scurry back to retrieve it. Such duels provided a spectacle of catching and kicking skills for the crowd.

But Jim Brough's claim to rugby immortality does not lie solely in his trusty left boot: his shrewd attacking play enabled him to play in the centre position on many occasions, not only for Leeds but also for his country. In an era renowned for static, strong-tackling, kicking full backs Jim Brough was the forerunner of the modern running style of full back play begun by Martin Ryan of Wigan after the War and continued by the likes of Ken Gowers, Austin Rhodes and Steve Hampson in recent years. Brough's tactical appreciation was rewarded when he became the first coach ever appointed to a Great Britain touring team in 1958. That side proved to be one of the most successful ever – the only touring side to score over 1,000 points – testimony to Jim Brough's attacking awareness.

OPPOSITE: *After hanging up his boots, Jim Brough brought his tactical awareness to coaching, with excellent results. Here he congratulates his Workington team after a Championship semi-final victory at St Helens.*

DAVE BROWN

b. 4.4.1913
Eastern Suburbs,
Warrington, Australia

Few spectators could fail to recognise Australia's prolific points-scorer, Dave Brown, thanks to his habit of wearing a scrum cap even though he played in the centre. There may have been little hair beneath the cap but there was certainly an abundance of rugby brain, for Dave Brown was one of the deepest of thinkers on the game and one of the most able of Australian Test captains. His amazing points-scoring feats in 1933–34, when he amassed a record 285 points on the Kangaroos tour of Great Britain, and his record 38 tries in a season and 45 points in a match for his club, Eastern Suburbs, gave him the credentials for consideration as the captain in the 1936 Test series. And he led his country in fine style when, in the first Test at Sydney Cricket Ground, he became Australia's

Dave Brown, who led Australia to victory in the first Test of the 1936 Ashes series, cuts an unmistakable figure in his scrum cap.

youngest captain at 23 years of age and helped to defeat 'th'aud enemy' 24–8. Although he was unable to rescue the Ashes from the British boys' grip such were his performances that he especially impressed the Warrington Test forward, Jack Arkwright, who recommended him to his club.

'Dave was a natural footballer who had a deceptive change of pace which fooled many a would-be tackler. He thought a lot about his rugby but his real strength was his tackling. He was a remarkable tackler and could topple the forwards despite his average 5 feet 9-inch and 12-stone 7-pound frame.' Jack Arkwright's praise indicates that Dave Brown had little to learn about the British style of play when he joined Warrington after the 1936 Test series. He remained at Wilderspool until the outbreak of the Second World War but, according to Jack, he always found the North of England a strange world. 'He had never seen a coal fire, I'm sure', Jack insists. 'He used to put the coal at the bottom and the sticks and paper on the top before attempting to light the fire. I think Dave found our winters a little colder than Sydney.'

When his playing days were over Dave Brown still had much to contribute to the welfare of Rugby League, and his deep thinking when on the field and his powers of leadership were put to good effect in his coaching and administrative roles. At his instigation a meeting of club coaches in Sydney in 1961 led indirectly to the eventual setting up of the modern Australian coaching system. Two years later he helped to coach the 1963 South African touring side led by former Springbok Union star Dave Ackermann. Sadly, despite Dave Brown's help, they won only two matches out of nine played on their Australian tour and the chance to promote League in South Africa was lost. Dave was an enthusiast both on and off the field and is rightly accorded his place as one of the greats in both countries.

CLIVE CHURCHILL

b. 21.1.1927
South Sydney, Australia

The press cuttings that followed one of the most entertaining Anglo/Australian Test matches ever, played at Headingley, Leeds in 1948, best summed up the awesome contribution this small, black-haired South Sydney full back was to make to Australian teams over the next eight seasons. Although Australia were defeated 23–21, Churchill's ability impressed everyone. Eddie Waring was moved to write: 'Churchill's running into the heart of the defence was cheekiness personified'; while 'D'Artagnan' reported in *Rugby League Review* magazine: 'He stood out head and shoulders above the rest. His fielding and touchfinding were well nigh faultless'. Such was his eye for an opening in attack, his steadiness when fielding a kick, and so deadly was his tackle that he not only achieved the distinction of playing in 13 Anglo/Australian Tests and 33 internationals for Australia in total, but also, between 1950 and 1954, became the only captain to lead Australia into nine Tests against Great Britain.

Although he was a small man, only 5 feet 7 inches in height and weighing approximately 12 stones, Clive Churchill had a powerful kick and could gain vast distances with his long range touchfinders. His tackling was also impeccable and indeed bone-shattering, as Stan McCormick, the Great Britain wing in that famous 1948 Test, declares: 'Clive was the best full back I ever had to beat. He was a deadly tackler; he hit you very low. He nearly snapped my legs in two with the impact from his shoulders when I was playing for Lancashire v Australia in 1948. I faced him in three Test matches and whenever I broke away he always had an uncanny timing to stop me. He was much faster than most full backs I had to face'.

Whether with the Souths club in Sydney, for whom he was voted Player of the Year in 1950 and 1952 and whom he later led to four Sydney Premierships as coach, or whether captain of Australia, he proved the perfect leader. It is no accident that both he and Jim Sullivan, skipper of Great Britain nine times in pre-War Tests, led from full back. Such a position, at the back of play, allows a player with vision the chance to assess the fortunes of tactics in front of him and enables him to watch the form of players attempting to employ the tactics. A full back can see the possibilities for attack opening out in front of him and can soon realise where there are problems in his own side's defensive system; it is the ideal position from which to captain a side.

British fans had few opportunities to see 'The Little Master', as he was known Down Under, in action. Workington Town made him a huge £10,000 offer to join them following that momentous tour of 1947–48, but Clive could not return to England. Like many of his fellow countrymen, he fell foul of the transfer ban which operated between Australia and Great Britain.

OPPOSITE: *Headingley, 1948. Clive Churchill leads the Kangaroos onto the field for one of the most celebrated Tests to be played on English soil.*

DOUGLAS CLARK

b. 2.5.1891
Huddersfield, Great Britain

In the first 30 years of the breakaway code of Rugby League such were the number of scrummages and the amount of tackling to be done in midfield by the forwards that it was taken for granted that anyone who opted for a career in the pack was tough. Few came harder or more gifted than World Champion Cumberland-style wrestler Douglas Clark, whose 16-season stay at Fartown is synonymous with the Huddersfield club's incredible success in the years surrounding the First World War.

Duggie Clark signed for £30.00 from Brookland Rovers, an amateur club, in 1909 and helped the famous Yorkshire club to three Challenge Cup victories and five Championship finals. A versatile forward, playing either at loose forward or in the second row, he toured Down Under on both the 1914 and 1920 tours, taking part in nine out of the ten Tests played against Australia and New Zealand, a remarkable feat of endurance for a forward. His career is even more amazing when one realises that during the Great War he was gassed twice, suffered blindness for a period and was in fact discharged at the end of hostilities with a 95 per cent Disability Certificate.

He will always be remembered for his bravery in the famous 'Rorke's Drift Test' of the 1914 tour. A week before the third and deciding Test almost half the team was injured, but Harold Wagstaff, the captain, was told by the Rugby League Council that he must take on the Australians. His battle-scarred side took to the field, but with ten minutes to go the team had been reduced to just ten men. Duggie Clark had broken his thumb in the first half but had remained on the field. In the second half his collar bone was broken and, although he was forced to leave the field twice for strapping, he played on in considerable pain until he could no longer continue. In his skipper's words: 'He had tears in his eyes when he left the field for the final time'. But he had played his part in enabling Great Britain to clinch the series by winning 14–6. In view of all his difficulties and those of his team it is fitting that the Test has come to be known as the 'Rorke's Drift Test', named after the famous battle in which British soldiers, although greatly outnumbered by Zulu warriors, fought a magnificent rearguard action.

Harold Wagstaff claimed later that, in his opinion, the Test was won by Duggie Clark the night before when his strong sense of humour helped to raise the spirits of the downcast team. On the eve of the Test match Duggie hid a six-foot snake in a cardboard box in the room of Walt Guerin, his team-mate. Unfortunately the snake, not content to lie peacefully in its cardboard box, decided to squirm its way out of the room and down the corridors of the hotel, much to the panic of the other residents and especially the manager. Order and humour were finally restored when, on returning to bed, Walt Guerin found the reptile curled up asleep in his pyjamas.

An entertainer both off and on the field, Duggie was the complete forward of his day. He was a master at the art of the 'dribble', a skill which is no longer seen in the League code and which faded out in Union during my playing days in the 1950s. His try in the third Test at Villa Park, Birmingham in 1912 came from such a dribbling of the ball at his feet after he had first broken from the No. 13 position. The tactic was to wheel the scrum while retaining the ball at one's feet, and then dribble the ball as fast as possible upfield. There was no better exponent of it than Douglas Clark.

Duggie Clark – World Champion Cumberland wrestler and one of the heroes of the Rorke's Drift Test.

NOEL CLEAL

b. 16.10.1958
Eastern Suburbs, Manly,
Widnes, Australia

One of the virtues of Australian club and international selectors is that they have yet to be influenced by the British concept, especially current in the 1970s and only now losing favour, that forwards under the six tackle and handover rules have to be much lighter than those of yester-year. Back three forwards in England are now often the size that big centres used to be because of an all-out effort by club coaches to inject speed into the pack. The British seem to have adopted the principle that if a man is of outsize proportions then he will be unable to run fast and will be lacking in co-ordination. Not so. Have our selectors never looked at some of the huge American Footballers who cover the pitch at great speeds? Or have they never appreciated the effect of Noel 'Crusher' Cleal as he rampages around the field and destroys the keenest of defences with his powerful, surging runs?

Anyone watching Noel Cleal's midfield runs in his Man of the Match performance at Elland Road, Leeds in the second Test of the 1986 Kangaroo tour could not fail to be impressed by the strength and speed of this ex-country boy. Noel is one of the few forwards who is so big and strong at 6 feet 1 inch and 16 stones that he can break the cover often at the first charge. In the tight, defensively-minded style of play in the Sydney competition such players are invaluable. His woolly beard gives an even more frightening look to a player who, apart from a liking for bumping opponents out of the way, lists his hobbies as fishing and wild pig hunting.

Sadly, his outstanding performances on the 1986 tour of Europe were brought to an early halt when he broke his arm at the Boulevard, Hull – an occupational hazard for players of Noel's style. On account of his rough and rumbustious play he has suffered many injuries which have cost his Manly club dear in recent seasons. Off the field Noel remains the quietest of characters with an even temperament far removed from that of the wild-looking 'man from the outback' on the park, where his performances have brought him to the attention of so many since he first joined Eastern Suburbs and came under the influence of coach Bobby Fulton.

His days as a centre in that first season at Easts certainly helped him maintain his edge in speed. But it is at Manly, again under the coaching of Bobby Fulton, that he has emerged as one of the leading forwards in the world and has become the cornerstone of the pack in the second row since his arrival in 1983. A brief spell of 16 guest appearances with Widnes, during which time he recorded eight tries, allowed a few English club forwards to appreciate the reasons why he is fondly referred to as 'Crusher'. His method of running through or over a player, rather in the manner of a steamroller, is a simple but an effective one. Unless you happen to be on the receiving end!

OPPOSITE: *The rough and rumbustious 'Crusher' Cleal sets up yet another Australian attack.*

ARTHUR CLUES

b. 2.5.1924
Western Suburbs, Leeds,
Hunslet, Australia

The finest pair of rugby boots I ever wore was given to me by a kindly, jovial sports shop owner by the name of Arthur Clues whose shop, situated just below the Leeds University buildings, was the haunt of most of the rugby-mad students of my varsity days. Sadly for Arthur those boots, surely an inducement for me to transfer my allegiances from Union to Leeds Rugby League, didn't do the trick, but I have never lost my respect and admiration for the larger-than-life character who epitomises Australian and Leeds Rugby League.

Full of fun and endowed with a sharp sense of humour off the field, Arthur Clues' rugby career was eventful to say the least. As a young 16-year-old with the Parramatta Rugby Union Club in Sydney he was banned for life from Union for a wild, impetuous act. Arthur was running touch for a match in which his sister's boyfriend was hit by another player. He threw down his flag and immediately set about the attacker. Thereafter he took up Rugby League, joining Western Suburbs as a First Grade player at the tender age of 17 years. For one so young, Arthur Clues had a heavy physique: blessed with a height of 6 feet 2 inches and a weight of 15 stones, few wanted to argue with him. However, his dismissal from the field when playing for Australia in the third of his three Tests against Great Britain in Sydney in 1946 is testimony to the fact that some did. His fiery clashes with the famous French forward Edouard Ponsinet when Arthur was playing for the 'Other Nationalities' team during the 1949–53 period is further evidence of his tough approach to forward play. But this should not detract from his other qualities.

By the time Arthur Clues left Australia to join Leeds, making his debut on 1st February 1947 against Hull, his performances in the 1946 Test series Down Under had stamped him as a player of the highest class. He was renowned as a constructive, ball-playing second row forward and a scorer of tries. He was exceptionally agile for such a big man and his 74 tries in the Leeds colours indicate what a dangerous attacking runner he was. His successful conversion to the British style of rugby was immediate, and within only seven matches of his arrival in Yorkshire he was lining up at Wembley in the Challenge Cup for Leeds against their rivals Bradford Northern. Sadly, the occasion, on which Leeds lost 8–4, was to prove the most disappointing moment of Arthur Clues' long and eventful career.

Although he played with distinction for two seasons (1955–57) for the other League club in the city of Leeds, Hunslet, it is at Headingley, where, as a player and later as a club director, he is best remembered. And not only for rugby – Arthur's skills were equally appreciated on the ground which adjoins the Rugby League pitch at Headingley, the famous cricket ground. Any sports quiz lovers should note that Arthur Clues is the only man to have scored a try and a century at both Sydney Cricket Ground and Headingley.

OPPOSITE: *Australian Arthur Clues displays a rugged defence for the Other Nationalities.*

LIONEL COOPER

b. 18.2.1923
Eastern Suburbs,
Huddersfield, Australia

Eddie Waring will always be fondly remembered as a household name in Britain, thanks to his unique and highly entertaining Rugby League match commentaries on B.B.C. Television. What many fail to realise is the deep commitment he made to the sport by way of his career in journalism and the work he did for clubs. Huddersfield is one club which will be forever grateful for his intervention on its behalf when he toured in 1946 as the first journalist to cover fully a Great Britain trip. Without Eddie Waring's help Lionel Cooper, Huddersfield's block-busting wing, might never have worn their famous claret and gold jersey with such distinction.

When Lionel, the powerful Eastern Suburbs and New South Wales wing, was selected to play in the first Test match held after the Second World War, Huddersfield approached Eddie Waring to help them secure his services. Lionel Cooper's display in that Test increased the urgency of Eddie's mission. With ten minutes of the match remaining Cooper levelled the scores at 8–8. He had received the ball after good passing along the threequarter line and raced 70 yards to score. A quick discussion with Mr Waring soon indicated that Lionel was willing to travel to Yorkshire, but he wanted a colleague to accompany him. It was to Eddie Waring's credit and an indication of his rugby knowledge that he persuaded Johnny Hunter, a fine full back, to join Cooper at Huddersfield and obtained the services of both for a mere £1,500. The pair repaid that fee many times over.

The big, bustling Cooper was the leading tryscorer at Huddersfield for seven seasons, scoring 432 tries in his career at Fartown and in season 1951–52 achieving the amazing total of 71 tries, only 9 tries short of the world record set by his predecessor and fellow countryman on the Huddersfield wing, Albert Rosenfeld. His ten tries in the match against Keighley in 1951 is still a club record.

Lionel was a big wing, tipping the scales at 14 stones, and he didn't mind whether he ran through his opponents or round them. For such a big and strong man he had a fine turn of speed and was completely fearless when going for the corner. I had no hesitation in including Lionel Cooper in my selection of 100 greatest players, but it is a tribute to the quality of Huddersfield's wingers that I can say only that he was one of their best. Has any club produced six better than Lionel Cooper, Mick Sullivan, Albert Rosenfeld, Peter Henderson, Ray Markham and Stan Moorhouse? I doubt it. Whatever the merits of each, Huddersfield's great forward Ben Gronow, who in his capacity as player and later as chairman at Huddersfield saw them all play, considered Cooper to be the best: 'They were all different types. "Rozzy" had a quick dart, a strong run, a short sidestep and a kick over the full back's head to gather and score. Lionel had a determination of his own'.

OPPOSITE: *Lionel Cooper demonstrates his famed hand off on one of his powerful runs down the wing for Huddersfield.*

MICHAEL CRONIN

b. 28.6.1951
Parramatta, Australia

Many Australian First Grade players in the Sydney Premiership become strongly attached to their adopted clubs but they rarely lose their affection for the teams of their early upbringing. Many re-visit the town team of their youth to present end-of-season players' awards or attend annual reunions in clubhouses sprinkled the length and breadth of New South Wales and Queensland. Few had or have the attachment that Gerringong's Michael Cronin maintained for his home town and team. Indeed, it took the Parramatta club many seasons to persuade him to leave the New South Wales Country League of Group 7 with Gerringong and take up residence in Sydney. Even though he returned home from the 1973 Kangaroo tour of Great Britain as the highest points-scorer on the trip with 77 points from 12 matches the lure of Sydney was not strong enough.

Michael Cronin was never happier than when he was playing alongside his brothers, John and Terry, for the Wollongong Christian Brothers or later the Gerringong team with whom he won the Group 7 League competition twice in 1970 and 1972. But it was inevitable that someone with his talent would eventually play in a more competitive atmosphere. At almost 6 feet in height and over 14 stones in weight he had the physical attributes to be a strong-running and hard-tackling centre. He was also a prolific goalkicker, a priceless asset.

When Parramatta finally secured Michael's signature he was to prove the bargain buy of the 1970s. In 1978 he scored 282 points for the 'Eels', as the Parramatta club is nicknamed, before going on to shatter the Test records with his tryscoring and goalkicking prowess. In the first Anglo/Australian Test match of the 1979 home series he kicked ten goals to equal the individual Test record of 20 points. In the same series he went on to total 54 points from two tries and 24 goals to establish a Test series record. It is little wonder that this modest yet gifted centre threequarter won the prestigious Rothmans Medal, awarded by referees to the best and fairest player in the Sydney competition, in two consecutive seasons in 1977 and 1978.

As I have explained elsewhere, the goalkicker who approaches the ball from directly behind it needs to have a considerable strength in the thighs as well as an accurate eye. Michael Cronin was one of Australia's most consistent goalkickers, having the strength and power to loft a ball prodigious distances and to great heights, always adopting the 'straight on' method. Not for Michael the 'round the corner' style much in vogue in the 1980s. Michael says of his approach: 'I set the ball on the lace as I found I could get more distance that way.'

Ask any of the Great Britain tourists of 1979 for the truth of that statement, for he broke their hearts with his performances in all three Tests.

Michael Cronin, often the pivot of Australia's midfield, seeks support from his Kangaroo colleagues.

LEE CROOKS

b. 18.9.1963
Hull, Western Suburbs,
Balmain, Leeds, Great
Britain

What can one say of a forward who had achieved all there is to be gained in a Rugby League career by the tender age of 19 years? Only that his precocious talents have not faded, as they often do with youngsters who suddenly burst onto the League scene – on the contrary, he has matured into one of the finest ball-playing props and tactical kickers of the 1980s.

Signed from Ainthorpe Youth Club by Hull as a 17-year-old in September 1980 as part of a local recruiting drive by the Humberside club, Lee did not take long to impress the faithful fans in the Boulevard's famous 'Threepenny Stand'. Although he enjoyed a fine start to his professional League career in the Hull Colts side and captained the first ever Great Britain Colts tour to Australia in 1982, his impact was made almost immediately in the first team. Indeed his debut in November 1980 against Salford, barely six weeks after his signing, heralded a hectic four seasons on the east coast. By May 1982, at the age of 18, he had gained a Challenge Cup winner's medal by playing a full part in that memorable replayed final at Elland Road, Leeds, helping Hull to defeat Widnes 18–9 and grabbing a try and three goals for himself. October of that same year saw Lee achieve what many considered to be impossible: a Test cap as a forward against the might of Australia at the record age of 19 years 42 days. An incredible feat when one considers the size, strength, ruggedness and experience usually considered necessities for forwards in Test rugby.

Yet this young forward was not lacking those qualities on his debut, appropriately made in Hull at the soccer ground at Boothferry Park, and such was the impression made on the Kangaroos then and on tour with Great Britain in 1984 that the Sydney clubs were soon queuing up for his services. Those clubs, Western Suburbs and Balmain, recognised the rarity of his talents in the modern style of rugby. Two summer stints with Wests and one with Balmain between 1985 and 1987 highlighted the Australians' search for an old style British forward who revelled in ball distribution as Brian McTigue, Brian Edgar and Vince Karalius had done in previous eras. The modern style of forward play, requiring all-purpose athletes who can run quickly and tackle, produces few creative artists. Lee Crooks, at 6 feet 1 inch and 15 stones 4 pounds, has the frame to do just that. The art of the ball distributor is to be able to stand up and ride the tackle that seeks to put him to the floor and even attract two or three would-be tacklers around him. Such a tactic helps to create the vital gaps in the defence and allows the forward, with clever sleight of hand, to pass the ball out of the tackle to a supporting player able to race through the gap. Lee switches the direction of play with great vision and often opens play out wide with a long pass to the backs.

To add to those skills Crooks has other key weapons in his armoury. His powerful touch-finding kick and ability to loft a high 'up and under'

OPPOSITE: *Great Britain's*
youngest-ever forward, Lee
Crooks, spearheads a
forward drive for Leeds.

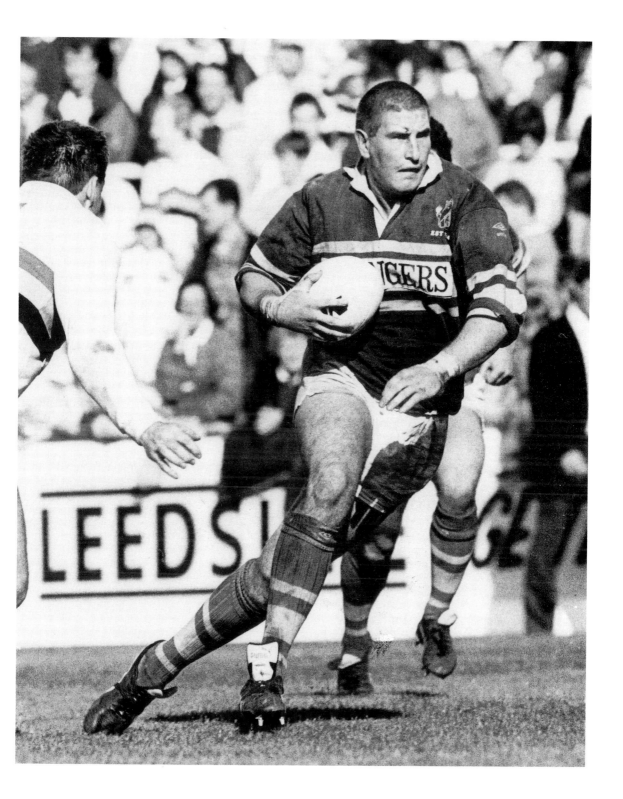

can cause havoc in the ranks of the panic-stricken defenders; as a goalkicker, when he is on form, there are few more powerful kickers of a ball. I well remember the drama and tension when, as B.B.C. Television's commentator, I had to describe to millions of viewers his last-minute kick in the third Test against New Zealand in 1985 at Elland Road, Leeds. The Kiwis were leading 6–4, and were within seconds of taking the Test series 2–1 when Lee Crooks displayed his cool, calm approach in equalising the score with a splendidly struck penalty goal from the touchline.

Such ability is obviously at a premium, and when Hull struck financial problems in 1987 it came as no surprise that in June Leeds paid a transfer fee of £172,500, then a world record, for Lee Crooks' services. Sadly, he was out of action for six months of the season due to a badly dislocated shoulder, which also cost him his certain Test place on the 1988 Lions tour. Such misfortune has now, it is to be hoped, been put behind this still-maturing young forward.

DES DRUMMOND

The fitness of modern Rugby League players was never better illustrated than when Leigh's black wing star Des Drummond achieved national fame in qualifying for the finals of the B.B.C. *Superstars* event in Hong Kong. This popular television programme, which attracted athletes from all sports in a contest of running, jumping and strong-arm feats, amply demonstrated the two qualities that have helped Des become an accomplished performer on the Great Britain wing. His pure speed and acceleration off the mark meant that there were few sportsmen who could match him over 100 metres in the heats of the competition back in 1983. And his strength, amazing for such a small man, gave him the endurance to defy others in the gruelling physical events. That strength and speed, in combination, made him a lethal finisher of movements down the wing. He was a most difficult opponent to stop, bouncing from tacklers like a rubber ball and bursting forth with tremendous acceleration when in the clear. Nor was he shy in the tackle, using all the expertise of his black belt judo training to topple and thwart the biggest of opponents.

b. 17.6.1958
Leigh, Western Suburbs,
Warrington, Great Britain

Des Drummond sails over the tryline, beyond the reach of his airborne opponent.

Although he toured Down Under with Great Britain in 1984, where he scored 11 tries in 17 appearances, his career began in humble circumstances. In 1975 Des joined the Leigh Colts team, having been persuaded to play in an Alliance League match when the team were one short. This would not have happened had he not accompanied his brother, Alvin, who was playing for the Leigh Alliance team, on the coach trip to the ground. His performance was so impressive that he was signed immediately after the match before any other club learned of his undoubted talents. He could not afford to celebrate his signing with champagne, however – the signing-on fee was only £25.00! This princely sum proved a worthwhile investment during Drummond's ten seasons with Leigh and his international career of six seasons.

Des has made a habit of reserving his best performances for the Test match arena. A prime example was his two-try effort in the third Test in 1980, which salvaged a drawn series for Great Britain against New Zealand. His two Tests in that 1980 series marked the start of a long international career, thankfully resurrected by Warrington coach Tony Barrow in the summer of 1987. Passing through Bolton, Des's birthplace, on his way to work, Tony Barrow noticed a forlorn figure jogging around the streets. It was Des Drummond attempting to keep fit, having been out of rugby for over 12 months as a result of a dispute with his Leigh club. A snap decision, a £40,000 fee to Leigh and Des Drummond resumed his career with Warrington, where his form touched such heights that he was once more invited to tour with Great Britain in the summer of 1988. Sadly his involvement in a dispute with a spectator during a match at Widnes shortly before he was to accompany the 1988 tourists Down Under led to disciplinary action by the Rugby Football League, which cost him his place.

GRAHAM EADIE

When Australian international Graham Eadie announced his return to Rugby League with Halifax in 1986 after almost three years in retirement, the Sydney press, and a few observers of the British rugby scene, declared that he was mad to even contemplate the idea. It was a tribute to the determination and fitness of this greatest of full backs that within 12 months of his arrival in the small Yorkshire town, perched high on the Pennines, he was to become their last line of defence in their Silk Cut Challenge Cup final victory over the mighty St Helens by 19–18. Furthermore, his impeccable display of full back skills was to gain him the coveted Lance Todd Trophy for Man of the Match at the age of 33. Not content with that distinction, the following year he was back again to face the star-studded Wigan side, sadly this time to pick up a loser's medal. Although he lacked a vital yard in pace Graham's positional sense and timing during those two seasons with Halifax were evidence of all the experience gained in his 17 seasons of rugby since journeying from Woy Woy to join Manly-Warringah in 1971.

The scouts who scour the junior teams of New South Wales never spotted better talent than the 5 feet 10-inch, 14-stone full back who burst on to the Test scene at only 19 years of age. As a youngster on his first Kangaroo tour in 1973 he proved to be a very strong runner into the threequarter line, joining many an attack out wide on the flanks and often scoring tries himself. He had the strength to shrug off the cover tackles of forwards but always had the sharp footballing instinct to look for a man better placed than himself. The hallmark of class full back play is the ability to burst into the gap, to make the extra man, but to hold onto the ball only long enough to allow the covering defenders no time to catch the player who ultimately receives the pass. The No. 1 must also be watching play from his deep position on the field and re-shaping tactics accordingly. Graham Eadie, in a coaching manual for youngsters, once wrote: 'A full back can watch the plays like a chess player and assess the opposing strengths and weaknesses. Temperamentally he must be a cool customer. He must not dither.' His own words are the best estimation of Graham's own ability.

Graham's contribution to Australian rugby, both at club and international level, was immense. He enjoyed two Kangaroo tours to Britain in 1973 and 1978 as well as World Cup experience in 1975 and was awarded 14 Test caps for Australia. In domestic rugby few Sydney clubs have ever had a more prolific points-scorer than Manly's Graham Eadie. In between 1971 and 1983, when he played his final game for Manly, 'Wombat', as he was affectionately known to the fans, scored an amazing 1917 points in First Grade rugby. It is little wonder that Chris Anderson, Halifax's Australian coach, tempted him out of retirement and allowed him to give the Yorkshire fans a sight of the player who graced the

b. 25.11.1953
Manly, Halifax, Australia

Graham Eadie, pictured during his short stay with Halifax, works to keep the attack flowing.

Sydney Premiership for so long. Many players who try to recapture their lost youth often end up by tainting their reputation. Not so, Graham Eadie. If it was ever possible, he added to his reputation as a magnificent full back.

BRIAN EDGAR

Brian Edgar, a Cockermouth Grammar School product, was one of a once rare breed of player which entered Rugby League at 18 years of age, having first represented England Schools at Rugby Union. Such players in the 1950s and '60s were few, although today, with the expansion of Rugby League in schools and the growth of comprehensive education, many full League internationals like Shaun Edwards (Wigan), David Stephenson (Leeds) and Mick Burke (Oldham) have since made the transition. Edgar was selected to play in the second row against Barrow in the Challenge Cup final of 1955, despite having signed professional forms for Workington only in January 1955, and having made only three first team appearances. Nor did he let them down – Town beat their Cumbrian neighbours 21–12.

b. 26.3.1936
Workington Town, Great Britain

The first Test of Great Britain's 1962 tour to Australia, in which the visitors overwhelmed the Kangaroos 31–12. Gentle giant Brian Edgar is treated to a tackle from Ian Walsh.

61

Brian had the physique to dominate in his usual prop forward position but he was blessed with a fine turn of speed which allowed him to make the type of break usually reserved for second rows. Indeed, he was able to play in the second row on many occasions both at club and Test level such was his adaptability. Above all, he had a fine pair of hands and a sense of timing with his pass that could cause havoc with the tightest of defences.

His era demanded from a prop forward both tight scrummaging and open running skills, for it was a period that straddled two distinct styles in the game of Rugby League. Twenty years before Brian Edgar's emergence as a top prop forward the second Test between Great Britain and Australia of 1936 had produced 75 scrums, almost one a minute. In the three Test matches of the 1984 Ashes series there were only 41 scrums, one every six minutes. Brian had the skills to have played in either era.

His talent was best shown on his three Lions tours abroad where he proved a model tourist, despite a slight hitch before he finally boarded the plane for his first trip in 1958. The manager, Tom Mitchell, had fought hard to have Brian included in the party of players but, in spite of a huge row between Mr Mitchell and the selectors, Brian Edgar was omitted from the list. Only when Oldham's second row, Sid Little, dropped out did the gentle giant from Cumbria join up for the first of his three tours. His second trip, in 1962, was followed in 1966 by his being awarded the captaincy of Great Britain in all three Tests against Australia when the original Lions skipper, Harry Poole, fell ill. His extra quality of leadership made him a natural replacement, but he saw success in the series snatched away only by the slightest of margins.

SHAUN EDWARDS

In 1983, in the early days of B.B.C. breakfast television, viewers were taken into the lounge of Mr and Mrs Jackie Edwards to see their son Shaun signing professional terms for Wigan Rugby League Club. The negotiations between the Edwards family and the Wigan coach, Alex Murphy, had been carried out in secret and the television cameras had been invited to await the ceremony at the stroke of midnight on Shaun's 17th birthday. Such a celebrated signing of a League and Union international, at a world record fee for a schoolboy signing of £35,000, naturally aroused the public's interest but the question as to whether Wigan's bold gamble would succeed has now been answered emphatically.

Within four years of his signing for the Lancashire club Shaun Edwards had achieved all there is to achieve in Rugby League and shattered a few records along the way. His fee on the transfer market would now be approaching six times the figure he received as a teenager. On 1st March 1985 Shaun, having already represented the Under 21 and Colts sides, became the youngest ever Great Britain Test player when he was selected to play at full back in the victory over France. He had gained the remarkable distinction of representing his country at Test level at the age of 18 years and 135 days. Not content with having won every conceivable medal with Wigan he crowned his 1984 feat of becoming the youngest ever player to appear at Wembley, at the age of 17 years and 202 days, by returning in 1988 against Halifax as the youngest ever captain to lift the Silk Cut Challenge Cup. At 21 he was the captain of a club that had developed greats like Jim Sullivan, Joe Egan and Eric Ashton. What foresight was shown by the Wigan management who invested their capital in him and recognised his talent and potential as a schoolboy!

Shaun's understanding and knowledge of the game is now such that, at only 22 years of age, he can control a match from his stand off position. Usually accompanied by his Wigan scrum half partner Andy Gregory, Shaun is at the centre of all the attacking play, whether launching his threequarter line with shrewd passes or sending forwards through the defensive gaps with short, sharp passes. And should he himself see a gap in the opposition ranks he has the speed off the mark and the instinctive footballing brain to take advantage of it. When playing scrum half for Great Britain in the win over France at Headingley in 1987 he produced that blistering pace away from the scrum to completely outflank the French midfield defence. Noticing that the French loose forward had moved from the scrum to cover the blind side, Shaun Edwards immediately attacked the open side, producing two neat sidesteps to beat the opposing scrum half and full back before placing the ball beneath the posts for a try, displaying speed, rugby craft and instinct all in one tryscoring run.

b. 17.10.1966
Wigan, Great Britain

Under the handover rule introduced in 1983, whereby the side in possession hands over the ball to the opposition after the sixth tackle, the art of kicking has been restored as a major part of a team's tactics. Shaun Edwards is a master tactical kicker, whether kicking to touch with his long, raking grubber kicks or using his chip kick over an opponent's head. These ploys have been used to good effect by Wigan coach Graham Lowe to break down the tightest of midfield defences. It is so refreshing to see a player prepared to kick the ball, and risk losing possession, to set up a surprise move or attempt to vary tactics. His wide-ranging talents have led to the selection of Shaun Edwards, a Great Britain tourist Down Under in 1988, in four different positions for his country. Whether at full back, centre, scrum half or stand off this 5 feet 7-inch, 12-stone Wigan-born youngster has filled his place with distinction and often with a most welcome element of surprise.

OPPOSITE: *Widnes v Wigan, 1984. Shaun Edwards, the youngest-ever player to appear at Wembley, rose to the occasion whenever he was needed to run the ball out of defence.*

JOE EGAN

b. 19.3.1919
Wigan, Leigh, Great Britain

The amateur side St Patrick's in Wigan has produced many outstanding players for the professional ranks, notably present day Great Britain stars Andy Gregory and Joe Lydon. But few have achieved the reputation of the club's most famous protégé, Joe Egan, the Wigan, Leigh and Great Britain hooker of the immediate post-War years. Having signed for Wigan as a 17-year-old full back in the January of 1937 Joe Egan, sadly, was robbed of many seasons' play by the outbreak of the Second World War but, once hostilities had ceased in 1945, he embarked upon

Joe Egan – the only hooker in the history of Rugby League to command a world record transfer fee.

a career that made him the highest-priced player in the game by 1950. For a hooker to command the record transfer fee from Wigan to Leigh of £5,000 (the only occasion in the history of the League code that a No. 9 has done so) is testimony to his ability, an ability acknowledged by his presence on two British Lions tours to Australia and New Zealand in 1946 and 1950.

Joe's career at Wigan coincided with one of the greatest periods in the history of the famous Lancashire club. The highlight for Joe was no doubt becoming the first man to receive the Challenge Cup from a reigning monarch, King George VI, after Wigan defeated Bradford Northern. Both at Wigan and at Leigh, where he became the player-coach in 1950, he played under the unlimited tackle rule, in existence until 1966, whereby a team could retain possession of the ball for an unlimited number of tackles until they created an offence. Such a rule, as opposed to today's limit of six tackles before the ball is handed to the opposition, created the need for huge 16- and even 17-stone forwards to command the midfield with powerful drives. And Joe Egan, although only 5 feet 9 inches in height, provided short or long defence-splitting passes for such forwards to run onto.

As forwards were thus able to command possession for lengthy periods Joe Egan developed into an astute ball player, specialising in his distribution of the ball and not forgetting his 'dummy', which sent many a defender the wrong way. His generalship and control of a pack, whether in the scrum or out of it, earned him 14 Test caps before he retired in 1956 to take up the coaching reins, first at his old club Wigan and later, in the mid-1960s, with Widnes. His years as captain of Wigan and Leigh moulded him into one of the League code's finest coaches: he achieved four trips to Wembley with Wigan (three times) and Widnes in just seven seasons.

During my spell as a player with Widnes from 1967–71 I benefited greatly as captain from the coaching of Joe and owe much of my success as a pack leader to him. On those cold, wintry evenings at Naughton Park Joe would coach our pack on intricate ball work, always stressing the use of brain not brawn, always urging me to let the ball do the work. His skill in slipping the ball out of a tackle, the art of drawing a man and the mysteries of scrummaging were all passed down by the master in his softly spoken manner and were, on my part, gratefully received. He was a thinker on the game who always realised that Rugby League must be an entertaining spectacle if it is to prosper.

Perhaps his one regret in a career of unqualified success was his failure to persuade Britain's famous Olympic sprinter, E. McDonald Bailey, to stop to entertain the crowds following his one and only appearance in Rugby League for Leigh in 1953. Despite a fee of £1,000 for the match, in which the black sprinter scored a try, even the persuasive tongue of Joe Egan could not convince him to stay any longer than 80 minutes in the tough atmosphere that Joe himself relished.

ALF ELLABY

b. 24.11.1902
St Helens, Wigan, Great Britain

But for a troublesome knee injury in 1926 which forced him to retire from playing soccer for Rotherham County (as they were then known) the exciting talents of Alf Ellaby might have been denied to Rugby League. That injury, though calamitous at the time, was to open up a new career for him as a flying winger, which established his worldwide rugby reputation. Indeed, the awe in which this St Helens-born lad was held in the town is illustrated by the story of a father who took his rugby-mad son along to see the stained glass windows at the local church. On explaining that they depicted some of the greatest saints who had ever lived, his son asked: 'Which one is Ellaby?'

Ideally built for a winger at 6 feet and 13 stones, Alf Ellaby certainly found his niche in life on leaving his first love, soccer. In over 290 appearances with St Helens from 1926 to 1934 and from 1937 to 1939 he scored 278 tries, an amazing strike rate. When we add his tries scored for Wigan between 1934 and 1937 and those scored on representative duty then his career total of 445 tries places him among the top flight of wingers. Such was his impact on the glass town of St Helens that the club's directors dared not reveal if he was ever injured and unlikely to play. Such news was announced shortly before the kick-off when a youngster would walk around the perimeter of the pitch carrying a board on which were chalked the team changes. Only when the size of the crowd could not be affected by his absence was Ellaby declared not fit to play.

Although I never had the pleasure of seeing Alf Ellaby thrill the crowds with his swerving touchline runs I have come to appreciate his shrewd rugby knowledge in deep conversations with him at Lions reunion dinners or functions of the Saints Past Players' Association. His still upright stance and graceful movements hint at his direct, forceful running style which resulted in him touching down for 41 tries in only 28 appearances on his two tours of Australia and New Zealand in 1928 and 1932. Needless to say, he topped the tourists' tryscoring charts on both occasions but it was the manner of his scoring which later brought rapturous praise from two of his immortal playing colleagues. His phenomenal pace is alluded to by full back Jim Sullivan: 'He could make a full back look silly with his power of shooting away to leave the man grasping thin air'. Centre Gus Risman acknowledged the balance and poise of a superb winger: 'The finest winger I have ever seen. His taking of a high pass on the tips of his fingers was masterly, he would touch the ball forward with his hands and never lost speed.'

If one looks at the careers of most of the great wingers one rarely fails to find a long-standing partnership with a centre who, although often lacking true pace himself, is gifted with the instincts to serve a winger with the right pass at the right time. Doug Greenall and Tom Van

Alf Ellaby.

Vollenhoven and Eric Ashton and Billy Boston are two famous pairings that spring to mind, and there is no doubting that the wily ex-Pontypool Rugby Union centre George Lewis was responsible for many of the overlaps which led to some of Alf Ellaby's most spectacular tries. He is best qualified to pinpoint Alf's ability to beat a man, which enabled him to record an amazing 31 hat tricks for St Helens: 'He would run up to his opposite winger, stutter, half stutter, but never stop running. He went outside his man all the time. Only once have I seen him come inside and then he left the great Jim Sullivan on his backside'.

Legendary wing Alf Ellaby and his Great Britain team-mate, full back Jim Sullivan, are eager to take advantage of a mistake by the opposition Down Under.

NEIL FOX

b. 4.5.1939
Wakefield Trinity,
Bradford Northern, Hull
Kingston Rovers, York,
Bramley, Huddersfield,
Great Britain

When Neil Fox was forced to pull out of the 1968 World Cup squad in Australia with a knee ligament injury there was no one more disappointed than myself. While I was overjoyed at my own selection, I knew that we had lost a scoring potential unequalled in the history of Rugby League and a player whose 14-stone frame struck fear into the opposition whenever he thundered upfield from his centre position. Neil's appetite for the game, spanning 23 seasons from his debut for Wakefield Trinity in April 1956 at 16 years of age until his retirement in 1979, never wavered. It was never satisfied while there were points to be had or caps to be added to his 29 international appearances, and it led him into coaching the Underbank amateur club when his playing days were over.

In a staggering 828 appearances at club, county and international levels he amassed a total of 6,220 points, consisting of 358 tries and 2,575 goals (including four one-point drop goals) – figures which, under modern rules, will surely never be beaten. Winning all the major trophies with Wakefield Trinity he gained the distinction of creating a Challenge Cup final individual record of 20 points in Wakefield's 38–5 win over Hull at Wembley in 1960. His try and three dropped goals in his side's defeat of Huddersfield two seasons later resulted in him being awarded the Lance Todd Trophy for Man of the Match.

One particular goal, struck by Neil Fox's sturdy left foot, confirmed for me his ranking among the greatest of goalkickers. In a torrid Championship play-off final in 1968 between Trinity and St Helens Neil Fox was given a chance to level the scores with a kick from the touchline. Amid pools of standing water on the touchline and in the teeming rain he placed the ball with undue care, all at Headingley having given up hope of the kick being successful. As he commenced his approach to the ball there was the most violent peal of thunder followed by a searing flash of lightning. Yet such was his total concentration that he never wavered in his run up and struck the ball with deadly accuracy between the posts. What an artist!

Although his bulk demanded that he moved into the forwards later in his playing career at Bradford, it is as a centre that he will best be remembered. As would be expected of such a big player, he was able to burst through tackles at will and possessed a strong defence himself. Yet he was also fast and like Mal Meninga, the great Australian centre, he was nimble on his feet and possessed delicate hands. Neil was an old fashioned centre whose first aim was to feed his winger with the right pass at the right time and he rarely failed to do just that. He was a thinker on the game and always aware of the tactical complexities necessary for success.

Even being one of that rare breed of men who somehow manage to play professional Rugby League beyond the age of 40 years did not

satisfy Neil's ambitions. His coaching of the Underbank amateurs and his organisation of many charity matches displayed an all-consuming passion for rugby. He was deservedly awarded the M.B.E. for his services to the sport.

The concentration shows as Neil Fox aims to add yet another goal to his mammoth haul.

BOBBY FULTON

b. 1.12.1947
*Manly, Eastern Suburbs,
Warrington, Australia*

Bobby Fulton was the one that got away, for if his parents had remained in the town of his birth, Warrington, then surely he would have ranked as one of Great Britain's best centres or stand offs. Instead, because of the greater opportunities offered Down Under at the time, Mr and Mrs Fulton Senior decided to join the many thousands emigrating from the North West of England to the warmer climes of Australia. And how his adopted country must thank them for that decision!

Australia gained a stand off with razor-sharp acceleration away from the scrum and with the physical strength to race through the arms of any half-hearted tackler. He was a strong tackler himself, often performing the role of an extra loose forward whenever he played at stand off for his club or country. His game was based on dedication to training and fitness, and this shot him to fame as a young stand off in the 1968 World Cup and the Kangaroos tours of Europe in 1973 and 1978, the latter as captain. That first tour illustrated a strong aspect of Bobby's play: he was hungry for tries. He scored 16 tries to become Australia's top tryscorer in only 11 appearances. It was on that first tour that he scored a try in the third Test which helped to clinch the Ashes, ironically in the town of his birth. It was indeed a strange quirk of fate that the only Test match to be played at Wilderspool, Warrington in the 80 years of competition between Great Britain and Australia should take place when a certain Bobby Fulton was playing. The weather on that day was intensely cold and the ice everywhere was enough to make anyone feel like emigrating.

The shorter move from Wollongong to join the Manly club in Sydney in 1966, when Bobby was 17, was to prove the key to his long and illustrious career. In ten seasons he guided the club to three Premierships, captaining them in his third in 1976 against Parramatta. In 1973 it was his two tries against Cronulla that turned the tide in his club's favour and helped them through to win the Grand Final. He moved to Eastern Suburbs as captain-coach in 1976, remaining with them until 1979, and enjoyed a short off-season spell with Warrington, but it is as a Manly player and coach that he is best remembered. His love affair with Manly did not end when he had completed the last of his 216 First Grade matches for them – after three seasons with Eastern Suburbs as coach he came home in 1983 to Manly, where he has continued to display the all-consuming passion of his playing days. The thirst for success he showed in his team's Grand Final triumph in 1987 also remains undiminished.

Though born in England, he was a typical Australian stand off, rather in the mould of one of his predecessors in the green and gold jersey, Vic Hey. Tough and uncompromising in his play, he has brought similar attributes to his coaching role.

OPPOSITE: *The Kangaroos' Test stand off Bobby Fulton shows Great Britain's full back Ray Dutton what it means to be 'Down Under'!*

JEAN GALIA

b. 20.3.1905
Villeneuve, France

The premature death of Jean Galia on 18th January 1949 at the age of 43 years robbed France not only of one of its greatest players but also one of its leading administrators and the guiding spirit behind the introduction of Rugby League across the Channel. Jean Galia's burning enthusiasm for the new game in the early 1930s and his defence of it during the Second World War helped to establish the League code in France against all the odds.

Born at Ille-sur-Têt, 15 miles from Perpignan in the heart of what is now League country, Jean Galia had represented Toulouse and Villeneuve at Union and had gained 20 international caps before any thoughts of Rugby League entered his head. Ironically, it was the R.F.U at Twickenham that provoked Galia to seek pastures new! The English Rugby Union, having chosen to sever connections with France over allegations of professionalism, indirectly caused many French players and clubs to look to the 'other game' that was flourishing in Great Britain. So when Jean Galia's club, Villeneuve, was suspended for poaching players from Perpignan Rugby Union Club, the 6 feet 1-inch 13 stone 7-pound forward was at a loose end – thankfully, not for long.

Soon afterwards Australian entrepreneur Harry Sunderland staged an exhibition League match between an Australian and an English team at the Pershing Stadium in Paris in December 1933. Jean Galia and some of his fellow Union players arrived to watch. He was enthralled by the spectacle, and within three months he had brought France's first Rugby League team to play matches at Wigan, Leeds and London Highfield. Such was his enthusiasm and that of those gathered around him that by August 1934, *rugby à treize* had begun in France with 12 founder clubs, Villeneuve, captained by Galia, emerging as the first champions. It was an incredible series of events considering that nine months earlier Jean Galia had never witnessed a League match. More incredible still was that France, under Galia's direction, won their first International Championship in 1939, only five years after their founders watched their first ever match in Paris. The dominance French Rugby League would have held today if officials, sympathetic to Rugby Union, had not banned the game under the Vichy Government of Marshal Pétain in 1941, can only be guessed at. Sadly the game's finances were confiscated and its city teams dissolved, but the fervour for the new code was kept alive in the remote villages where even today it retains its biggest impact.

Jean Galia was a tireless worker off the field and on it he was a natural leader blessed with the usual fiery Gallic temperament, but he adopted a highly disciplined approach to his team. The ex-amateur heavyweight champion never shirked the tough encounters in the pack, could run and handle a ball in the manner of a classy threequarter, but his greatest

Jean Galia, the driving force and inspiration behind the French Rugby League in its infancy in the 1930s.

contribution to French rugby in the immediate post-War years was leadership. He, more than anyone, paved the way for the golden era of French rugby in the 1950s. John Wilson, then secretary of the Rugby Football League, summed up Galia's ability and his contribution to French rugby: 'He was one of the best attacking forwards I have ever seen, even though he was at the end of his career when he turned to *rugby à treize*. He was a real captain, very necessary in a French team. He once hauled a team-mate from the pack in a match at Headingley and boxed his ears for a misdemeanour'.

REG GASNIER

b. 12.5.1939
St George, Australia

Reg Gasnier was christened 'Puff the Magic Dragon' by the Australian press because of his uncanny ability to evade the grasp of any tacklers. He well deserved that title for he was blessed not only with a fine physique to cope with the demands of centre play but also possessed a burst of speed that could leave the opposition floundering. Some great players have an enormous array of skills, some have the combination of size and speed that can prove so devastating in back play, yet very few have had the balance when running of Reg Gasnier which, for me, made him the greatest of Australian centres. His change of pace deceived many a player who thought he had him well within his sights; his swerve fooled many a full back who trailed to the corner a yard slower; his sidestep put many a defender on his backside. Not only was he a great individual but, especially in partnership with his big, blockbusting co-centre, Harry Wells, he was the ideal centre for a winger to play outside, such was the accuracy of his passing and his timing when releasing the ball. In all of his 36 appearances in the green and gold jersey Reg Gasnier gave few ordinary performances.

From his early schooldays, when he excelled at both Rugby Union and cricket, his promise heralded an extraordinary career. After barely four matches in the Second Grade for St George in 1959 he was included in the First Grade matches and within weeks his skill had tempted the international selectors to give him his international debut in the Test series against New Zealand that season. It was success all the way for the talented Reg, but nothing matched the sensational impact he made upon the British scene when he arrived as a much-lauded young hopeful with the 1959 Kangaroo tourists. By the time he and his colleagues had left the British Isles his reputation as one of the finest centres ever to touch an oval ball was confirmed.

On his sensational debut in an Anglo/Australian Test at Swinton in 1959 he recorded a hat trick of tries and destroyed the reputations of the Great Britain centres Alan Davies and Eric Ashton. Wherever he went he was to prove the centre of attraction and the British fans could barely wait for his return on the next tour of 1963. Why they were so eager to see him again I'll never know for, as one who played against him on that Kangaroo tour, I can testify to his single-minded destruction of our Test hopes. A further hat trick of tries before the Duke of Edinburgh in the first Test at Wembley gave him the distinction of being the first player to perform that feat twice in an Anglo/Australian Test match. His five tries in the series also gave him the record, alongside Australia's wing star Ken Irvine, of most tries in a series. Some player!

Sadly his third tour of Britain, as captain in 1967, was to end in disaster. He broke his leg in the first Test at Headingley and took part in only five matches throughout the trip. Only 1,000 people saw him attempt a comeback on the French section of the tour when he played at Avignon on 21st December. He limped off the field having aggravated his original leg injury – a sad exit for a player who graced the game as a gentleman and gave pleasure to untold millions throughout the world with centre displays of the highest order.

Reg Gasnier outwits Great Britain's David Bolton as he races on for a try.

KEN GEE

b. 23.9.1916
Wigan, Great Britain

An estimation of the impact made by Ken Gee both on the opposition and the spectators can be gauged by a tale told by Ken against himself. Having been continually alerted to the hardships in England and the malnutrition caused by food rationing, the Australians had sent thousands of food parcels to the mother country in the months immediately following the end of the Second World War. Imagine, then, the surprise of one Aussie supporter on seeing Ken Gee and his fellow prop Frank Whitcombe enter the Sydney Cricket Ground on the 1946 Lions tour

Powerful prop Ken Gee battles across to lend his weight to his harassed Wigan team-mates.

'When we came down the steps of the cricket ground for the first Test Frank and I were carrying a combined weight of 35 stones and, as we got to the pitch, an Australian sitting in the first row of seats shouted, "Look at these two fat Pommie props, and we thought there was supposed to be a famine in England".'

Ken, at 17 stones and 5 feet 10 inches, was a colossus of a prop in an age when few pulled the No. 8 or 10 jersey over their heads if they weighed under 16 stones. In the 1940s and '50s, in a game played under the unlimited tackle rule and with no differential penalty, the scrum figures would often mount as high as 60 per game. And really big men were needed to absorb all the punishment of so many scrums. They had to dominate the midfield of play, win the ball and know how to use it in short, driving runs down the middle or in short defence-splitting passes to colleagues in support. The packs of a Rugby League match resembled two stags locked in battle in a test of brain and especially brawn. And Ken Gee, with over 33 international appearances to his credit in a 21-year career with Wigan from 1933 to 1954, was the outstanding prop of his era.

In partnership with hooker Joe Egan, both at club and international level, he forged a reputation for solid scrummaging based on a physique of powerful shoulders and massive thighs. He, more than anyone, played his part in achieving total dominance over the Australian and New Zealand packs on the tours Down Under in 1946 and 1950 and his play fully justified his 17 Test caps. Yet such was the abundance of talent in the 1930s that, in common with many other players of his era, after his signing in 1933 he had to mark time for two seasons in the Alliance team before he finally broke into the Wigan first team. It is not only for his forward play that Ken Gee is renowned, for he was also a prolific goalscorer.

In my school days I grew up watching giant forwards like Harry Bath (Warrington), Harold Palin (Warrington) and Vic Yorke (York) kicking long distance goals and dominating the goalscoring charts. In my playing days forwards of the calibre of Kel Coslett (St Helens), Terry Clawson (Leeds) and Jim Fiddler (Leigh) figured prominently in the lists. Not so today – one rarely finds a forward taking the kicks at goal, perhaps because the pace of the game is so much faster for a forward, perhaps because they are so much lighter in weight than the forward kickers of yesteryear. Whatever the reasons, there is no denying the attributes which made Ken Gee such an accurate marksman. His 133 goals in season 1949–50 (he topped the goalscoring charts with another forward, Harold Palin) came as a result of a steady eye and a powerful kick.

Such was the fame and respect for the giant prop in his native town of Wigan that today the Ken Gee Cup tournament for all the local amateur League sides in the borough is held annually in his honour. And it is a fitting tribute, too, to the cornerstone of the invincible Wigan team of the late 1940s.

MARK GRAHAM

b. 29.9.1955
Otahuhu, Norths Brisbane,
North Sydney, Wakefield
Trinity, New Zealand

New Zealand Rugby League has always laboured in the shadow of the national Union side, the All Blacks. Whatever great players they have produced in the past the public's consciousness for League has never quite matched that of its counterparts in Britain or Australia. Perhaps the fact that New Zealand League is an amateur game, even at the highest levels, is an important factor in determining the public's appreciation of it. Nevertheless, by the end of 1985 the League version held the public's imagination in the land of the long white cloud for the first time in the history of the two rival codes. This was entirely due to the efforts of the Kiwi international team led by their giant 6 feet 5-inch and 16-stone captain, Mark Graham. During that memorable season he emerged as the finest second row in world rugby and his Kiwi Test team as arguably the best of the five nations competing at international level.

Mark Graham's performance in the third Test of 1985 against Australia, when the Kiwis won 18–0, was flawless. His bursts down the middle led to many New Zealand attacking positions, his deadly cover tackling kept Australia without a point on the scoresheet and his captaincy proved inspirational to the other 12 players under him. Although, owing to ankle ligament damage and a depressed cheekbone, he appeared on the Headingley pitch for only half an hour in the first Test of that same year against Great Britain he wrought havoc with the opposition. The final score, 24–11 to New Zealand, was surely due to his efforts in those vital opening 30 minutes. He stood head and shoulders above everyone else on the pitch and led by example. His pass to Gary Prohm allowed winger Dane O'Hara to score at the corner, and in the 26th minute he strode between the posts to score himself. He had controlled the match and before his departure through injury had won the game for the Kiwis.

Mark first played League as a six-year-old at St Joseph's convent before going on to captain Otahuhu, represent Auckland and become the only New Zealand player to captain two tours to Great Britain in 1980 and 1985. But it was his elevation to the professional ranks in the highly charged, competitive atmosphere of Australia which was to sharpen his skills and produce the best second row in the world. The amateur concept of New Zealand Rugby League has hindered their performances at Test level but, now that their best players, once they have played in two Test series, can journey overseas and play professionally, the outlook at international level is much rosier. Current Test players Kevin Iro, Adrian Shelford, Shane Cooper and Dean Bell have all secured lucrative contracts abroad and then returned home to advance the Kiwi cause at international level. Mark Graham was one of the pioneers of this practice.

After his brief stay with Norths in Brisbane his wholehearted style of play attracted the rich clubs of Sydney and in 1981 he began his lengthy

OPPOSITE: *Two Warrington*
defenders struggle to stop
giant Kiwi Mark Graham
passing the ball out of the
tackle.

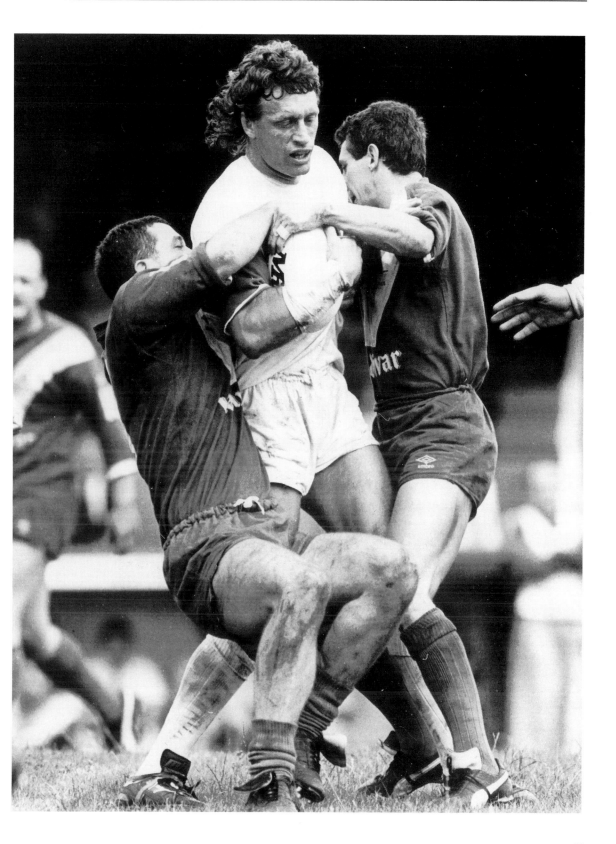

career with North Sydney. Naturally he was soon made captain of the club. His leadership on the field is due, in part, to his sheer physical presence, but his tactical awareness is also high. For one so tall, he possesses a fine turn of speed which he uses to good effect in his last-ditch cover tackles, and that speed also helps him to an average of just less than one try for every two international matches played – an impressive record for a second row forward.

DOUGLAS GREENALL

Duggie Greenall, who gave every ounce of his $10\frac{1}{2}$ stones to the cause of St Helens Rugby League Club from 1944 to 1960, was once described by Gordon Hughes of the *Daily Mirror* in unflattering fashion: 'The face looks like an ordnance survey map. The limbs are bent, gnarled and twisted like an old oak'.

b. 7.6.1927
St Helens, Wigan, Bradford Northern, Great Britain

That description highlights the terrible physical punishment which Duggie's frail body suffered both in taking and in delivering some of the hardest tackles I have ever seen on a rugby field. He broke virtually every bone in his body and was feared by all who faced him for his lethal tackling. He was Desperate Dan and Flash Gordon rolled into one to the youngsters who, like myself, crowded into the Boys' Pen at Knowsley Road to see him perform his defensive feats.

Even the Australians, usually the toughest of characters, feared him and, following a series of clashes between Duggie and Noel Hazzard in the centre positions, even accused him of wearing a plaster cast on his elbow to 'stiffen' his opponents. When he arrived Down Under for the Great Britain tour of 1954 he was greeted at Darwin Airport by banner headlines in the newspapers announcing 'The Bad Man arrives today'. It was all quite unnecessary and undeserved publicity, but understandable to anyone who was ever tackled by him. He would fell 15-stone giants like logs with a perfectly timed tackle, flying through the air from the side. Wrapping his arms around the player he would envelop him and bring him instantly to the ground. They were David and Goliath clashes but David, or Duggie, always won.

'Premier', writing of his exploits in a Test match against New Zealand, perfectly captures the suddenness of the tackle and its effect on Baxter, his New Zealand opposite: 'Baxter was running in line to take a pass from the slim but aggressive Menzies. The ball arrived as expected. So did Greenall as expected, by us, if not by Baxter. The Kiwi hit the turf with a wallop'.

This tackle was unique to Duggie and according to the Great Britain centre himself was perfected in the immediate post-Second World War years at St Helens: 'We had a very weak side and as a youngster, only 17 years old, I was playing on the wing. I used to hide at the side and would come in to stop the stand off from moving the ball along the line for another try. Keeping the score down developed my style'.

But Duggie Greenall was much more than a defensive centre, he was one of the most creative players and sharpest of thinkers I have ever seen grace a threequarter line. He had the task of nursing the legendary St Helens wing Tom Van Vollenhoven into the Rugby League code when he transferred his allegiances from Union. He did it in style and rarely gave the flying winger a pass that did not create a chance for a score. He was an inspirational captain, setting an example to his colleagues.

Challenge Cup medals and Championship medals came his way with regularity, but he was never accorded the honours he deserved, gaining only 6 Great Britain caps in almost 20 seasons of play.

Duggie skippered Wigan in 1961–62 and spent a short period as player-coach to Bradford Northern but the St Helens-born lad, educated at Rivington Road School, was most at home on his beloved Knowsley Road ground. His comments at the end of his career on the subject of his ludicrous signing on terms as a 17-year-old – a payment of £30.00 with a stipulation that he played six first team games before the money was handed over – best sum up his love of St Helens Rugby League Club: 'If the stipulation had been 60 games I would still have signed for the Saints'.

Bradford, 1951. Having split the New Zealand defence, Great Britain's centre threequarter Duggie Greenall steams in for the home side's third try.

BEN GRONOW

When Huddersfield, 'the Team of all Talents', lined up to face St Helens in the Challenge Cup final of 1915 they needed only victory in that match to compile Rugby League's Grand Slam by winning all four trophies available at the time. Naturally at that final, which they won easily 37–3, all attention focused on their great threequarter line of Rosenfeld, Gleeson, Wagstaff and Moorhouse as it had throughout the season. But, as in any League side, before the backs can do their job the forwards must take control. In Duggie Clark and Ben Gronow the Fartown side had two of the finest forwards in the world at that period. Not only did Ben Gronow kick five goals in that Challenge Cup final but he scored 136 goals in the season, a figure he beat with 148 when he topped the goalscoring charts again in 1919–20.

b. 3.3.1887
Huddersfield, Batley,
Featherstone Rovers, Great
Britain

Ben Gronow, signed by Huddersfield for £120 in 1910, was one of Rugby League's many catches from the Union code.

Having signed for a fee of £120 in 1910 this ex-Welsh Union international joined Huddersfield from Bridgend at a time when they were the finest team in the land and, with such stars playing alongside him, it was not long before Ben won the first of his seven Great Britain caps in 1911. Sadly the First World War intervened and many opportunities for further honours were missed after Mr J. Platt, the secretary of the Northern Union (as Rugby League was then called) declared that, 'serving King and Country is more important than winning medals on a football field'. Nevertheless, when hostilities ceased and the Rugby League grounds stopped being used as recruiting and drill areas, Ben Gronow established himself as the ideal forward, even attracting his own fan club in the 1920s.

He was selected for the two Lions tours of 1920 and 1924, in the former displaying outstanding form by kicking 65 goals and scoring 2 tries in only 16 appearances. Ben had a huge appetite for Rugby League – and he needed it. For on those tours he was paid just 75p a week while at sea and only £2.00 a week when on land, hardly an incentive to give up one's job for six months.

An immensely strong forward, he was naturally renowned as a fine scrummager, a skill very much in demand in those early days. He was a powerful tackler and a runner with a very effective hand-off. He also kept himself very fit to enable him to do all the chasing upfield for the ball which forwards had to undertake in his playing era. And he was nimble on his feet for such a big man. Forwards had to be skilled with their feet for the manner of the play the ball in those days meant that the ball had to be dropped from waist height with both the player dropping the ball and his marker being allowed to kick at it. Ben Gronow's tactic was to perform a little drop kick to a man alongside him, for the ball did not have to pass between the legs as is necessary today.

ERIC GROTHE

Eric Grothe, the 14-stone Parramatta and Australia winger, once spoiled one of my dreams and I believe he was the only winger in the world who could have done so at the time. After 25 minutes of the third Great Britain v Australia Test in 1984, when the Lions were leading 6–2 and seemed about to break the run of defeats Australia had inflicted upon them for six years, Eric Grothe intervened and dashed all our hopes and dreams of celebrating a historic win. There is a pleasant warm feeling and a glow of national pride from the British press corps whenever the Lions lead the Kangaroos and, fortified by copious supplies of warm meat pies and endless cartons of squash, pencil in hand, I was ready to write the glorious chapter when he struck.

Receiving a pass only ten yards from the Great Britain tryline, and hemmed in on the touchline, there appeared to be no way through even for a player of Grothe's size and speed. The British cover was streaming across and all seemed in control. Suddenly, with a burst of speed which belied a man of such size he rounded the despairing tackle of Garry

b. 6.1.1960
Parramatta, Leeds,
Australia

Leeds and Parramatta wing Eric Grothe fends off a cover tackler using his formidable hand off.

Schofield and, as if in the same movement, he crashed through the usually dependable arms of full back Mick Burke, himself a fine physical specimen of some 14 stones. Eric proved to be unstoppable once he had gathered momentum and that try, which I am convinced no other winger would have scored, launched Australia on the rampage and led them to a convincing 20–7 victory.

In that tryscoring movement Eric Grothe displayed all the attributes that have made him such an entertaining winger. Few opponents on the wing relish tackling a man of Eric Grothe's size and height (6 feet), especially one who is never afraid to take the direct route *through* the man to the tryline. Allied to his strength and size, he possesses a fine turn of speed which takes many a winger by surprise. He is a clever footballer too, as is indicated by the fact that coaches are able to use his services in the centre whenever their team plans are in trouble. And above all, like most great wingers, he has an appetite for scoring tries, his seven tries in the Tests against Great Britain and France on the 1982 Kangaroo tour demonstrating his ability to score at the highest level. With his flowing beard he presents a fearsome sight when hurtling down the wing and is hardly the man to be welcomed by any full back looking for a quiet day.

As a youngster, the quiet guitar-playing lad had represented the New South Wales Under 18 side before being asked to join Parramatta, who had been forced to rebuild their team at the end of the 1970s. Having scored 16 tries in 17 matches in the club's Under 23 side he was given his debut in the First Grade against Wests at only 19 years of age. Within three years he had risen to become Australia's premier wing on the 1982 tour of Europe and in the 1984 home Ashes series. Although he enjoyed an off season spell with Leeds in England he was troubled with knee ligament problems, an injury which has sadly restricted his club and international appearances in the past few seasons. But whatever he achieves in the future I will never forget that shattered dream.

ELLERY HANLEY

Any player who can play in four different positions at international level – centre, stand off, wing and loose forward – must have something special. Ellery Hanley certainly does. His attributes have made him the most sensational player and the biggest crowd puller of the past decade, and his feats on the field have made him one of the most consistent and spectacular tryscorers of all time, regardless of his position.

Signed by Bradford Northern on 2nd June 1978 from the Corpus Christi amateur club in Leeds, he waited three seasons before making his debut in his first full game for Northern against Halifax in August 1981. It was not an auspicious debut, but he did serve notice to the Rugby League world that what he loves to do best is to score a try. Tries, tries and yet more tries seem to be the order of the day whenever Ellery Hanley plays, and already in a career far from completion the records have tumbled. At Bradford Northern in 1984–85 he became the first player to score over 50 tries (55) since the legendary Welsh winger Billy Boston performed the feat in 1961–62. That figure was the highest ever recorded in the history of two-divisional rugby and the most by a non-winger, most of his matches having been played in the stand off position.

After his £150,000 record transfer from Northern to Wigan in September 1985 Ellery continued to lighten the gloom of many a wintry afternoon at Central Park with his incredible tryscoring feats. His 63 tries in that season proved to be the highest total ever by a non-winger and his 30 tries from 17 appearances in the loose forward position were yet another record. His old club Bradford Northern were to suffer at his hands when he set yet another tryscoring record against them in 1987, recording five tries from the No. 13 position, the only occasion a forward has achieved this in a Division One match.

Nor have all his best tryscoring efforts been at club level: on the 1984 tour of Australia where, surprisingly, he was played as a winger by his coach Frank Myler, he notched up 12 tries from 17 appearances. On the 1988 tour as captain, the first black player ever to achieve this distinction, he scored eight tries and led Great Britain to victory in the third Test over Australia, their first for ten seasons.

How does he achieve such totals and make such an impact upon a team? Ellery can play in either the forwards or the backs for he has all the attributes needed for both. He has pace, a sidestep, a devastating swerve and good handling skills. Allied to these he has a powerful physical frame with well developed upper body strength, so necessary for powering past forwards and for making the 30 or more tackles per match which is his norm. The free-roaming commission, when playing at loose forward, given to him by his Wigan coach Graham Lowe, and at international level by Great Britain coach Mal Reilly, allows him to enter the play wherever and whenever he wants. And also at the most

b. 27.3.1961
Bradford Northern, Wigan,
Great Britain

The spectacular Ellery Hanley hurdles Hull Kingston Rovers defender Mike Smith as he heads for the tryline.

unlikely times! Perhaps Ellery's greatest asset is his sense of positional play. His strength and speed can carry him through or around many would-be defenders but it is his instinct for a try which takes him over the line with such frequency. He has an uncanny ability to read a game, follow its movement and be in the right place at the right time when a colleague has made a break. He is at his best when finishing off a tryscoring movement from 30 or 40 yards.

ALAN HARDISTY

Somewhere in the small Yorkshire mining community of Castleford lies one conveyor belt which doesn't carry coal but supplies the professional Rugby League club with an unending seam of rich, young talent. Whenever the names of the club's internationals – John Joyner, Kevin Beardmore, Mal Reilly and countless others – are mentioned there is a common factor behind their success. Like Alan Hardisty, all acquired their skills and learned the basics of Rugby League in the club's Colts teams before parading on the world's stage. Lacking the glamour and wealth of some of the bigger League clubs, 'Classy Cas', as they are known, have relied on producing their own home grown talent and certainly in Alan Hardisty, their skipper and stand off for some 13 seasons between 1958 and 1971, they unearthed a nugget of pure gold.

b. 12.7.1941
Castleford, Leeds,
Rockhampton, Great Britain

Partnered at half back by Keith Hepworth, a gritty, combative type of player, Alan Hardisty proved the perfect foil with his silken skills and pure speed. Both earned their nickname of 'the H Bombs' for the devastation they caused all around the pitch for the opposition. Keith Hepworth was noticed for the whole of the 80 minutes, never short of energy and always busy around the base of the scrum, while Alan Hardisty ghosted in and out of a game at will.

With the finishing speed of a wingman and the electrifying burst off the mark of an athlete Alan was ever the calm, controlled master of all Castleford and Great Britain's operations in midfield. His tries were usually scored from two ploys which he had perfected to a fine art, though his sense of support play behind the pack brought him many more. Whenever I, as captain of either St Helens or Widnes, had the pleasure of facing Alan on a pitch there was always the danger of allowing my side to forget all about him at certain stages of the game. He would seem to be unconcerned with the proceedings on the field but then would strike when you least expected it and often in devastating and spectacular fashion. It was as if he could sense your attention wandering.

Alan toured twice Down Under, and two tries from his first tour illustrate his methods. In the first Test match at the Sydney Cricket Ground in 1966, when Great Britain defeated Australia 17–13, he helped his side to victory with a typical darting dash from the acting half back position before kicking over the Australian full back's head. Few could beat him in a chase for the ball to the tryline. Another try in the third Test of that series amply shows his uncanny knack of pouncing for interception tries, usually when the opposition were at their most dangerous. His interception of a pass intended for Australian full back Les Johns typified Alan Hardisty's perfect sense of timing, while his speed over the ground did the rest for the try: a brilliant opportunist and an entertainer who always played pure rugby.

Having skippered Castleford to two successive Challenge Cup

Castleford captain Alan Hardisty keeps an eagle eye on the Challenge Cup after his team's 11–6 victory over Salford in 1969. His half-back partner, Keith Hepworth (left) is, as on the field, in close attendance.

triumphs at Wembley over Salford and Wigan in 1969 and 1970 respectively Alan, for his services to the Castleford club, was allowed a free transfer to Leeds. It was a sign of his rugby knowledge and experience that, though in the twilight of his career, he was able to reproduce some of his best form to take Leeds to Wembley in 1972 and help them win the League Championship final as well.

ERIC HARRIS

b. 22.8.1909
Toowoomba, Leeds

Leeds is looked upon as a club which throughout its history has encouraged cultured back play and has rightly, on account of its traditional playing style, attracted some of the finest wingers to Headingley. Wilf Rosenberg, John Atkinson and Stan Smith are all class wingers who have thrilled the fans with their touchline dashes in the Leeds colours and yet none had the charisma of the import from the Darling Downs in Queensland, Australia.

Eric Harris, or the 'Toowoomba Ghost' as he was named after his birthplace and the manner in which he glided past his opponents as if they didn't exist, proved to be one of the best signings ever made by the shrewd Leeds committee. The 6 feet 2-inch, lean Australian wing was to prove a sensation from the very first match he played for Leeds in September 1930 against Featherstone Rovers, for after only ten matches he had recorded 29 tries for his new team. His instant acceleration past a player and devastating change of pace were to delight the Yorkshire fans for the next nine years until the outbreak of the Second World War necessitated his return to his native Queensland, where his athletic prowess enabled him to become the Director of Physical Education for the state.

The 'Toowoomba Ghost', Eric Harris, who found fame with Leeds, pauses for a moment's reflection before play begins.

In his first season in the British League Eric Harris was nursed into the Leeds side by another Australian, the experienced centre Jeff Moores, yet he needed little nursing. In his first season he scored 58 tries, topping the Rugby League's tryscoring charts, and was to top the lists on six occasions in his nine seasons at Headingley. Indeed, he is the only player to have finished at the top in four consecutive seasons. His tally of over 400 tries in nine seasons and his record of 36 tries in 17 consecutive matches in 1935–36 are testimony to his uncanny ability. He was able to escape the clutches of his opponents by seeming to dance out of a tackle. Many a time a player would feel he had a hold on the 'Ghost' only to find that he had escaped. Of course, his sheer speed was at the heart of his wing craft and Alfred Drewry, the highly respected *Yorkshire Post* journalist, pointed to his 'amazing ability to accelerate when he seemed to be going all out'. Such an ability was shown in what many consider to be his finest try.

In the Challenge Cup final of 1932, played at Wigan because Wembley was not available, Eric Harris made a decisive and cup-winning intervention when Leeds and Swinton were balanced at 8–8. Receiving the ball on the right wing he beat Swinton's left winger Kenny with ease and, as players covered quickly across field, he wisely kept to the wing despite the approach of the Swinton full back, Scott. The No. 1 was expected to crash Eric Harris over the touchline but, using his deceptive change of pace, he 'ghosted' past Scott for the winning try and the acclaim of the Leeds supporters who to this day rightly acknowledge him as the best winger ever to don their famous blue and amber jersey.

TOMMY HARRIS

To convince anyone watching a huge mound of rising steam enveloping a mass of outstretched legs and upturned faces that the gentleman in the No. 9 jersey is a specialist and a craftsman is a most difficult task. Yet the hooker at the centre of a League scrum needs to acquire such a high level of expertise that throughout the history of the League code it has been one of the most difficult of positions to switch to from Rugby Union. However, Tommy Harris, the ex-Newbridge Union hooker, mastered the skills to become one of the finest exponents of the art.

In Rugby Union the skill in scrummaging is to develop a tight shove forward, keeping the scrum parallel to the touchlines, with the props packing low and tight against their opposite numbers. In Rugby League the hooker, working in conjunction with a big open side prop who packs in a more upright stance, attempts to swing himself and the scrum around and onto the ball. The same eye for the ball and speed of movement in the legs is obviously needed in the League scrum as in the Union scrum but the whole operation demands a more physical approach.

Although only 5 feet 8 inches tall and 12 stones 10 pounds in weight, Tommy Harris had the strength and craft to develop his skills to the full, and like two other ex-Welsh Union hookers, Frank Osmond (Swinton) and Tony Fisher (Bradford Northern), he went on to represent Great Britain. Tommy gained 25 caps between 1954 and 1960, including nine against Australia, to become the most capped hooker of all time. In accompanying Great Britain in 1954 and 1958 on their tours Down Under he joined the select band of hookers (Peter Flanagan (Hull Kingston Rovers), Kevin Beardmore (Castleford) and Joe Egan (Wigan) are the others) that made two separate Lions tours. But Tommy Harris was not just a possession winner, he was a gifted footballer in the loose.

I well remember journeying across to Hull in the early 1960s to play against their dreadnought pack of huge powerful men such as the Drake twins, Mick Scott and John Whiteley. But it was the little hooker scampering around the play the ball situations who had to be watched closely, for he was the shrewd distributor for the powerful charges of the bigger men around him. The 69 tries scored by Tommy for Hull in his incredible 444 appearances for the club, between his first trial match in December 1949 and his last in 1962, are testimony to his eye for the gap and speed to shoot through it when close to the opposition tryline.

He was a tireless worker on the field and, whatever the outcome of a match, he always had a smile on his face, even during the most heated exchanges. And yet the one occasion on which even he found it difficult to raise a smile proved his greatest moment. It was a fitting tribute to Tommy's glorious career that he should have been awarded the Lance Todd Trophy for his Man of the Match performance in Hull's Challenge

b. 5.6.1927
Hull, Great Britain

OVERLEAF: *After his retirement Tommy Harris became a director of York. As a player he mastered the transition from Union to League in the most difficult position, at hooker, to become one of the finest exponents of the art.*

Cup final defeat by Wakefield Trinity in 1960. Although he was forced to leave the field twice for treatment and suffered severe concussion he battled on against ever mounting odds to become the only hooker to win this most coveted of Rugby League trophies.

Des Drummond
Varley Picture Agency

OPPOSITE: Malcolm Reilly
Varley Picture
Agency

LEFT: Eric Grothe
Varley Picture
Agency

Peter Sterling
Colorsport

Mark Graham
Varley Picture Agency

ABOVE: Ray Price
*Varley Picture
Agency*

RIGHT: Shaun Edwards
Bob Thomas

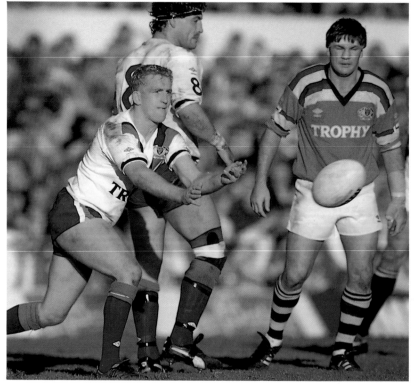

OPPOSITE: Graeme West
Colorsport

Roger Millward
Sporting Pictures (UK) Ltd

VIC HEY

Injuries to one player often provide the opportunity for another to break onto the international scene and launch himself into a glittering career. Some seize the chance for glory when it presents itself, others fail to make the most of it and sink back into anonymity. Vic Hey more than seized the opportunity to make a name for himself when, just before the Australian tour of Britain in 1933–34, E. Norman failed a fitness test. The Western Suburbs stand off was selected and went on to feature in six consecutive Anglo/Australian Test matches before signing for Leeds in 1937.

b. 17.11.1912
Western Suburbs,
Toowoomba, Ipswich
(Australia), Leeds,
Parramatta, Australia

At his peak in the mid-1930s Vic Hey weighed approximately 13 stones and was 5 feet 8½ inches in height. Such was the forceful nature of his play and his aggression in the tackle that one contemporary referred to him as 'a little bull'. Unlike many stand offs, he especially enjoyed tackling and often performed a role somewhat similar to that of a loose forward in that he liked to cover across the field behind his threequarter line when they moved forward to tackle their opponents. His style of movement across the field was akin to the role performed nowadays by a 'sweeper tackler' who lurks behind the first line of defence ready to cut down anyone who pierces the defensive line. Hey's advice was: 'Always follow the ball along the opposition to constitute a second line of defence'. Such was the strength and tenacity of the man that Gus Risman, the Great Britain captain, confesses to having put into operation a move at very short notice when he spotted in one Test match that Hey was injured and being treated. Such an opportunity rarely came Britain's way when Hey played.

Yet for all his defensive abilities he was signed by Leeds for his brilliant attacking play and especially for the way he could burst through a tackle using a combination of his immense strength and his speed off the mark. Few tacklers could hold him. He was described by the late Alfred Drewry of the *Yorkshire Post* as 'almost 14 stones of dynamic energy, as quick off the mark as a bullet, and with a sidestep like a fairy'.

At Leeds his fame helped the Yorkshire club to attract huge crowds to Headingley Rugby League ground and on one unique occasion to the cricket pitch which adjoins it. Few would believe that a Rugby League match has ever been played on the hallowed turf where Yorkshire's Boycott and Hutton scored their centuries and where Trueman and Bowes took their wickets, but a match did take place between Leeds and Salford at Christmas in 1938, when the League pitch was frozen hard. Vic Hey carved his name in the record books and the annual round of quiz questions in Leeds' 5–0 victory over Salford by becoming the only man to score a try on the Headingley cricket pitch.

Although he was born in Liverpool, New South Wales, it was perhaps fitting that Vic should complete his career in Britain in 1944 as the

Australian stand off Vic Hey, pictured during a training session, shows the formidable physique that enabled him to burst through a tackle with ease.

player-coach of Dewsbury, the town in which his father was born and where his family originated. After the 1939–45 War Vic enjoyed two further seasons of rugby with Parramatta where, as player-coach, he helped the fledgling club to make a start on its brief but glorious history in the Sydney League.

MARTIN HODGSON

The pack that toured Down Under with Great Britain in 1936 is considered to be one of the finest sets of forwards ever to tour Australia and New Zealand. Nat Silcock, Jack Arkwright and Harry Beverley struck fear into the opposite six wherever they played, and when Martin Hodgson, the rugged Cumbrian second row, is added to the line-up it is easy to understand how the Ashes were brought back to Britain.

Martin Hodgson began his rugby career with the Egremont Rugby Union Club but it was on signing with Swinton in Manchester that his rise to worldwide fame began. He was lucky in that he joined Swinton

b. 26.3.1909
Swinton, Great Britain

Martin Hodgson, Great Britain's strong-tackling forward, dashes across to cover a break by Australia's Wally Prigg.

in the 1920s, at a time when they and their local rivals at Salford were attracting crowds to equal those at their neighbouring soccer ground at Manchester United and Manchester City. But Martin Hodgson would have been a Great Britain player no matter which club he joined, for at 6 feet 1 inch and 17 stones he had the physique for the hard forward play of that era and he had the appetite to succeed. He excelled both in attack and defence, frequently making strong runs upfield, using his powerful hand-off to good effect and making bone-crunching tackles at either corner flag. Gus Risman, his colleague on the first of his two tours, in 1932, sums up Hodgson's contribution to the Great Britain side: 'He was a veritable rock of Gibraltar; tacklers rained off his broad back like dead flies. His cover defence was uncanny. Woe betide any winger cutting inside with Martin anywhere near'.

One of the features of his play was his speed about the field, exceptional for such a big man, and the perfect timing of his cover tackles. When an opposition movement was in full cry for the tryline Martin could somehow sense where a wing would receive the ball and would, much to the often fragile winger's surprise, be waiting for him at the corner flag. The winger was usually dumped unceremoniously over the touchline.

I have referred elsewhere in this book to the incidence of goalkickers who played in the forwards and Martin Hodgson was one of the most celebrated members of that select band. The modern goalkicker usually approaches the ball from the side, taking his run-up some yards to the right or left of the ball before hitting it, usually with his instep. The lighter rugby balls, which are coated with plastic and do not absorb rain and lightweight rugby boots in use today make this style appropriate in the modern game. It was not ever thus: in Martin's day the ball was made of leather and absorbed water from the pitch and boots were made of thick, hard leather with solid toe caps and high instep protection – hardly the equipment for flighting the ball delicately between the posts.

He was a prodigious goalkicker, approaching from directly behind the ball and kicking it with the toe cap of the boot. That he was successful and that he had immense strength in his legs can be judged by his tally of 65 goals on the 1936 tour and by his record for the longest goal kicked in any Rugby League match. His goal against Rochdale in April 1940 for Swinton is credited as being 72 metres long. Yet Martin Hodgson had little intention of scoring when he placed the ball – he merely wanted to use the penalty to waste a little time while the players of both sides cooled off after some heated exchanges. Instead he set a new world record!

Martin was a colossus of a forward in an era when Britain produced packs that were the envy of the world. It is an indication of his standing in those packs that he is still the only British forward to have played in five Anglo/Australian Test series, and is surely the only man never to have played on the losing side in 12 appearances against the Australians for Swinton, Cumbria and Great Britain.

KEITH HOLMAN

In the 1980s Australia's preference at scrum half has been for a small, wiry player, exceptionally able around the scrums, eager to make quick, darting breaks in attack and accustomed to covering the field at great pace to provide the link in free flowing movements. Such players as Peter Sterling, Steve Mortimer and Mark Murray rarely seemed to be tackled in possession and darted in and out of play rather in the manner of a dragonfly. Not so Australia's scrum halves of previous decades: Keith Holman, the chunky pocket Hercules from the Western Suburbs club, liked nothing better than to indulge in the close-quarter play in midfield and took great delight in stopping many a big forward with his crunching tackles. The fact that Keith played in the 1950s under the old unlimited tackle rule meant that as a scrum half he had to become involved in far more work around the base of the scrum than his modern counterparts and was expected to put in his share of the tackling.

Western Suburbs in Sydney has a remarkable record for producing scrum halves for Australia. Ex-Kangaroo skipper Arthur Summons and Tom Raudonikis came from the same stable, but Keith Holman was

b. 11.9.1927
Western Suburbs, Australia

The first Test of the 1952 Ashes series. Australian scrum half Keith Holman uses his pack as a shield as he attempts to place a kick into the corner.

Keith Holman.

without doubt their greatest No. 7. He was a battler (rather in the mould of my old friend and ex-international colleague Tommy Bishop) who liked to take the ball himself at the defence and often helped himself to a try or two in the process. In two Kangaroo tours of Europe in 1952 and 1956 he collected 13 tries in only 20 appearances. His work around the base of the scrum was second to none for with his 5 feet 6-inch and 12-stone nuggety frame he had the physical presence to shrug off any loose tackles by the opposition and he was intimidating to most other scrum halves.

In a record career for any Australian player of 14 matches against Great Britain between 1950 and 1958, he had many rave notices in the newspapers. But perhaps his best performance was his starring role in the first Test against France in Paris in 1956 when he helped defeat a very strong 'Chanticleers' side 15–8. Alex Murphy has no hesitation in naming Keith Holman as the best scrum half he ever played against even though he was in the twilight of his career when they met in the 1958 Test series and, by common consent, Murphy had the upper hand.

Many players, when they have retired, lose interest in the game, fading away from the rugby scene as though from a surfeit of rugby in their careers. Not so Keith Holman: after representing Australia in 33 Tests his appetite for the League code was as strong as ever and it is pleasant to record the effort he put back into the game. In 1961, under the influence of ex-Test centre Dave Brown, he helped to found the forerunner of the modern coaching schemes which have given Australia their premier position in world Rugby League. Not content with that, he helped to coach Western Suburbs and even graduated to Test class as a referee. Not only was Keith a man who gained much pleasure from Rugby League but also one who put much back into it for others to enjoy.

HAROLD HORDER

Unlike prop forwards or scrum halves who are usually of a certain physical mould, wingers tend to come in all shapes and sizes and display many varied skills and degrees of speed. Nowhere on the rugby field are there greater differences in style. Lionel Cooper liked to charge his way past the opposition; Kerry Boustead liked to employ his quick darting run to the corner; Cec Blinkhorn preferred to hug the touchline and use his pace to veer around his opposite number. Blinkhorn's wing partner on the 1921 record-breaking tour of Great Britain, Harold Horder, was short of stature, possessed a magnificent sidestep and swerve and liked nothing better than to switch inside from the touchline, cutting diagonally across the field to find a weakness in the defence. Harold's 35 tries and 11 goals on that 1921 tour stamped him as a winger of the highest class who, in the opinion of the mercurial Great Britain wing, Alf Ellaby, was 'comparable to any wing I have ever played against or seen play'.

b. 23.2.1894
North Sydney, South
Sydney, Australia

In an Anglo/Australian Test career of nine caps between 1914 and 1924, he was acknowledged as a prolific points-scorer, being a fine goalkicker as well as a regular tryscorer in club and international rugby. The year 1921 was certainly the pinnacle of Horder's career for, as well as amassing those 127 points when on tour with the Kangaroos, he scored 18 tries and 55 goals in helping his club, North Sydney, to their first Sydney Premiership in 1921.

Having toured New Zealand in 1913 with the New South Wales state side he made his debut for Australia in the first Test against Great Britain in Sydney 1914 but, like many players making their debut, his performance was such a disaster that it very nearly proved to be his last. Indeed he had to wait another six years before he had the chance to parade the full array of his talents on the Test stage. The Kangaroos' Ashes-winning series against Great Britain in 1920 saw Harold at his best – he created the winning try in the first Test for Frank Burge with a well judged cross kick and followed up with an accurate conversion of the try. In the second Test at the Sydney Cricket Ground he added another try and a goal in Australia's 21–8 victory.

Many wingers who are renowned as prolific tryscorers have tended to concentrate all their energies on attack and have often preferred to draw a veil over their defensive capabilities. Not Harold Horder: such was his tackling ability that he liked nothing better than to move infield, leave his wing position and stop an attack with a full blooded tackle on a centre or rampaging forward. He was the complete winger.

Horder was forced to retire in 1926 owing to a serious knee injury. However, he did not abandon the League code but continued to give great service to the game in Australia both as a touch judge and as a referee.

The short, stocky physique of Harold Horder, when allied to his considerable pace, made him a difficult opponent to stop.

WILLIE HORNE

b. 23.1.1922
Barrow, Great Britain

In the modern age of player contracts and increased mobility of players from club to club few spend their whole career with one team. This was not the case in the 1940s and '50s when men like Ken Gee (Wigan), Jimmy Stott (St Helens) and Willie Horne (Barrow) were associated only with the town in which they were born and for which they played throughout the length of their careers. The names of Willie Horne and Barrow are usually uttered in one breath, such was the impact made on the shipbuilding town by the classy 5 feet 9-inch, 12-stone stand off who led Barrow to their greatest triumphs in the 1950s.

From his early days at Risedale School and the Risedale Old Boys Under 19 teams Willie was destined for great honours, despite the frail appearance he offered to the opposition. He was one of those rare players who are naturally gifted at rugby and who have a vision on the field which is ahead of all others. He was a calm tactician, always thinking in the heat of battle and never forsaking the first priority of a stand off – launching his threequarter line into attack by clever ball distribution. Although he could sidestep and thread his way through the midfield he was the ideal stand off for a centre to play alongside. Phil Jackson and Dennis Goodwin, Barrow's two international centres, are proof of the effectiveness of Willie Horne's accurate, speedy passing. His ability to draw the opposition onto himself, thus opening a gap for the centres to run onto his perfectly timed passes, was masterly. His long passes flew like a bullet to the outside centre or wing with such timing that Stan McCormick, the master of the interception try, bemoaned the fact that it was impossible to intercept a pass off him, he was so accurate'.

Many television viewers will have heard me comment during a televised match on the vogue today for kicking a goal in the 'round the corner' style whereby the player approaches the ball from the side and kicks the ball with his instep. David Watkins, Paul Loughlin and Gary Pearce have all been kickers of this style. In an era when goalkickers approached the ball from directly behind and kicked it with the toe of the boot Willie Horne was unusual in that he very successfully pioneered the 'round the corner' technique.

Willie Horne's eight Great Britain caps and his two tours with the Lions in 1946 and 1950 are proof that brains can regularly get the better of brawn in Rugby League. He was a pure footballer and a leader *par excellence*, captaining Barrow in three Challenge Cup finals in 1951, 1955 and 1957. His calm approach when he scored five goals and a drop goal inspired Barrow to defeat near neighbours Workington Town 21–12. Willie's array of skills was never better demonstrated than when he teased and taunted a St Helens side in the Challenge Cup semi-final of 1956, helping to restrict the cup favourites to a 5–5 draw. As a teenager in that 38,897 crowd at Swinton I held my breath every time he ran

onto the ball or unleashed one of his long, raking kicks. We were thankful for the final whistle and the sight of the frail figure making his exit down the players' tunnel. But it was a sad day for Barrow when he made his exit from the club after a stint as player-coach, for they have rarely risen since to the heights which they achieved under the inspired leadership of Willie Horne, Barrow's favourite son.

OPPOSITE: *Skipper Willie Horne celebrates his biggest triumph: his club Barrow's capture of the Challenge Cup after beating Workington Town 21–12 in 1955.*

DICK HUDDART

b. 22.6.1936
Whitehaven, St Helens,
St George, Great Britain

One of the results of the introduction of the four and eventually six tackle rule in 1966 and the handover rule in 1983 (whereby the ball is handed to the opposition after the six tackles have been absorbed) has been the increase in strong-running, tryscoring forwards. Players like Bob Haigh (Leeds) and Bob Eccles (Warrington) took advantage of the greater freedom and increased running chances in midfield to top the tryscoring charts ahead of the backs. Prior to the 1960s forwards were not renowned for their exceptional tryscoring feats, their talents in the main being confined to tackling, scrummaging and clearing the trylines. However, one of a handful who proved the exception was my second row colleague at St Helens, the giant Cumbrian forward from White-haven, Dick Huddart. And what an exception he was!

Dick's tryscoring feats at the lowly Whitehaven club were first brought to international attention when he collected 17 tries for himself on the all-conquering Great Britain tour of Australia in 1958. But it was his play at St Helens, to which he was transferred on his return from that successful tour, that stamped him as a great attacking forward. In the early 1960s coaches were of the opinion that the ideal back row trio of a pack should be composed of a ball playing, skilful loose forward, one grafting, hard-tackling second row and another speedy, attacking second row. I had the honour to do a tackling stint for Dick over a couple of seasons and the pleasure to watch one of the greatest running forwards in action.

He had a powerful hand-off and made good use of his thighs in forcing defenders away from him. I can still see Dick running wide in an arc, swatting defenders off like flies with his powerful right hand, before straightening up for the inevitable try. It was also inevitable that, after winning the Lance Todd Trophy for his strong midfield bursts in the famous St Helens v Wigan Challenge Cup final in 1961 and after his 13 tries on the 1962 tour Down Under, he should be much in demand with the rich and glamorous Sydney clubs. His transfer to St George in the 1963–64 season robbed Britain of one of the finest sights in Rugby League, but at least his many fans in Australia were able to appreciate his powerful dashes down the middle. Great Britain acknowledged Dick Huddart's talents on 16 occasions but perhaps the best testimony to his inclusion in my selection of players comes from the man who usually packed down behind him in the scrum, Vince Karalius: 'He is the best attacking forward I have ever seen in my life. Tremendously strong. He knocked them off like ninepins'.

Dick's enthusiasm for the game could be seen when, despite being handicapped with a knee injury, he still managed a couple of his characteristic dashes down the middle in an exhibition match in Sydney in 1988 between former Great Britain and Australian players.

OPPOSITE: *St Helens'*
international second row
Dick Huddart displays the
speed of a threequarter as he
streaks upfield, setting a
Saints attack in motion.

BILLY IVISON

b. 4.6.1920
Workington Town

To meet Billy Ivison today, as I often do on the terraces of many a League ground, with his short, stocky physique, bald features and perpetual smile, one might think he is a kind, warm-hearted gentleman. And so he is – off the field. Once on the pitch, however, he was one of the hardest competitors, toughest tacklers and craftiest loose forwards it was ever my privilege to watch. That this stalwart of Workington Town never played for Great Britain in a Test team was a scandal but this does not change my opinion that he was one of the great constructive loose forwards of any era. Shame on you, selectors!

Billy Ivison began his career with Moresby Rugby Union Club in Cumbria before guesting with York in the Second World War. It was when Workington Town entered the Rugby League professional ranks in season 1945–46 that they realised they had unearthed a gem of a craftsman at No. 13 in this short, craggy Cumbrian. His defence was impeccable and his cover tackling of a wing on the run down the touchline was often timed to perfection. Yet Billy Ivison's speciality was his constructive work in midfield around the scrums and the play the ball situations where he wrought havoc with his delicately timed passes and his neat but devastating dummy.

Workington Town's loose forward Billy Ivison (right) indulges in some subtle obstruction to assist his scrum half's pass.

Since the introduction of the handover rule in 1983, the incidence of scrums has decreased considerably and much more play is begun in broken field situations rather than from endless play the balls. The opportunities today for loose forwards to become ball players, skilled in linking with their half backs around these set pieces, are thus far fewer and their style of play has changed as a result. Top international loose forwards such as Bob Lindner, Hugh McGahan and Ellery Hanley are invariably runners of the ball or support players. In Ivison's era a No. 13 had to be constructive and create play for the slower moving forwards around him and to blend into moves with the half backs. Billy Ivison was an artist in this respect. He could mesmerise the opposition with his quick thinking and deceptive switches of play.

While Workington Town had many gifted players in the early 1950s and achieved much within a short period of gaining full membership of the Rugby Football League it was Billy Ivison who was at the centre of their success. His grit and toughness were displayed when, despite suffering from a broken jaw, he helped Town to defeat Warrington 26–11 in the Championship final of 1951. His craft was never more in evidence than when he became the first Cumbrian player to the win the Lance Todd Trophy in his side's defeat of Featherstone Rovers in the 1952 Challenge Cup final.

Sadly the modern game provides too few loose forwards in the constructive mould but, as the late J. Hodgson, former Secretary of Workington, indicates, Billy Ivison was the complete master of the tactics needed for his own playing era: 'His movements worked from the base of the scrum split the best of defences wide open week after week; his guile from the play the ball could be equally devastating'.

GARRY JACK

b. 14.3.1961
Western Suburbs, Balmain,
Salford, Australia

When Salford flew Garry Jack 12,000 miles from the sun of Sydney to the mist and damp of a Sunday afternoon in Manchester to play rugby for them midway through the 1987–88 season, many pundits were of the opinion that either he or the Salford Chairman had gone mad. The player adjudged to be not only the world's greatest full back but also the greatest player in the Adidas Golden Boot competition in 1987 was leaving an Australian summer to join relegation-threatened Salford. Chairman John Wilkinson seemed to be wasting his money by bringing a world star to play before dwindling audiences at the Willows ground. By the end of the season, however, Garry Jack had turned in some sparkling performances, the attendances had risen appreciably and Salford avoided relegation from Division One. In fact Salford had done no more than continue their tradition of bringing world stars such as David Watkins and Keith Fielding to a club which has always had a touch of glamour about it. And the blond-haired speedster at full back certainly boosted that glamour, giving the Salford fans a sight of his speciality, his piercing runs down the touchline from the No. 1 position.

Since his days as an Illawarra junior player this dashing full back, who joined Western Suburbs in 1981 and Balmain in 1982, has liked nothing more than to catch the ball in a defensive situation and race upfield at great pace. The handover rule could have been designed for a player of Garry Jack's abilities. The solid tackling, slow moving but sure and steady full backs were suddenly at a disadvantage in 1983 as club coaches saw the need for a clever footballer who could use his speed and his safe hands to take advantage of the increased kicking in the game and the greater opportunities afforded for broken field running. Garry Jack uses his speed to take advantage of any misplaced kicks which come his way and, using his 13-stone frame to good effect, he is a difficult man to stop when on the run. The number of high kicks, or 'bombs' as they are known, which put the opposing full backs under pressure and avoid handing over the ball, was another result of the rule change. However this was of little use when Garry Jack was waiting underneath the ball. No full back today has safer hands for catching a ball when faced with would-be tacklers all around him.

In 1984 he captured the No. 1 position for the Ashes series against Great Britain and held the Australian full back spot for the New Zealand Tests, the Kangaroo tour to Great Britain and France in 1986 and the home series with Great Britain in 1988. His rock solid defence allowed the Kangaroos to attack at every opportunity, safe in the knowledge that all was secure behind them. His skill is such that he can easily link up as an extra man in the threequarter line. This causes enormous problems for the opposition full back and defence who have to cope with his fine bursts of speed.

OPPOSITE: *The adventurous Garry Jack likes nothing more than to link with his threequarters or set up a dangerous counter-attack.*

LEWIS JONES

b. 11.4.1931
Leeds, Wentworthville,
Great Britain

The 'Golden Boy', as Lewis Jones was known when he made his Welsh Union debut in 1950 at 18 years of age against England, was one of the most sought-after Union stars in the early 1950s. His performances for Neath, Devonport Services and Llanelli had elevated him at a tender age to the Welsh side and his displays for Wales and the British Lions on their tour of Australia and New Zealand in 1950 made him a natural target for the League scouts. When Leeds shocked the rugby world by tempting the slightly built Welshman to move north for a sum of £6,000, the Headingley ground was set buzzing with fans eager to see him perform.

Despite a compound fracture of his arm within two months of his signing in 1952, Lewis Jones was to rewrite the record books both for Leeds and Great Britain. On the 1954 tour he helped himself to a Test match record total of ten goals in the second Test at Brisbane and scored 278 points on the trip, a record at the time. In season 1956–57 he created a season's points record which still stands of 496 points (194 goals and 36 tries). For Leeds his 13 goals against Blackpool in 1957 and his 31 points against Bradford Northern in 1956 are still individual match points records for the Yorkshire club, while his 166 goals in 1956–57 still stand as the club's record total for a season. As a student at Leeds University and later as a player with St Helens I had the opportunity to watch and play against Lewis and I never failed to wonder at his talents.

He was the most relaxed of players, often appearing casual in his attitude. He seemed almost uninterested in the proceedings on the field of play, until he decided to attack and then his flair, pace off the mark and penchant for the unorthodox would take opponents by surprise. As well as a magnificent sidestep, he possessed a strange hitch kick with which he used to take himself past a would-be tackler. I have seen only one other player, Keith Northey of St Helens and Widnes, use a similar ploy. Jones' timing of a pass when in the stand off position launched his centres into the attack at top pace and those who believe that Gareth Edwards invented the spin pass should have watched Lewis Jones use the same technique when he wished to miss out a man. Opposition supporters used to highlight Lewis's supposed fault, an inability to tackle with genuine enthusiasm. But let me assure everyone that when Lewis wished to tackle there was no better cover tackler in the game and he always went for the legs of his opponent. He was a tactician with a ball in his hands and when he put it to his boot he could pin a side back with long, raking, touch-finding kicks.

It was at a very late stage in his career when in 1964, aged 33, he left England to join Wentworthville in Sydney as their player-coach. This surprise move by Wentworthville gave Lewis the opportunity to lead

the Sydney Second Division club to many a Premiership. Indeed his appetite for the game and fitness remained undiminished: his talents were still on display for Wentworthville four years later, when I had the pleasure of watching him play in a curtain raiser match before I was due to line up for Great Britain in the World Cup at the Sydney Cricket Ground. At 5 feet 10 inches, he still weighed 12 stones 10 pounds as he had when he first entered Rugby League with Leeds 16 years before.

VINCE KARALIUS

b. 15.10.1932
St Helens, Widnes, Great
Britain

I readily admit that the most frightening experience of my rugby career was not the actual move from Rugby Union to Rugby League in August 1961, but the prospect of meeting and playing alongside one of my boyhood heroes, Vince Karalius. I could not comprehend that my ability had been considered good enough by the St Helens management to play in the same team as this giant of the Saints and Great Britain pack. Whatever inferiority complex I may have had was smoothed away by this most perfect of gentlemen (off the field!) who, although he remained at St Helens for only a few months before his transfer to Widnes in March 1962, gave me all the advice and help any novice could have needed.

Like many other all-time greats Vince Karalius came to Rugby League only when he was invited to play for an amateur side which was short of players. However, once he had joined the local West Bank side in his native Widnes it was only a matter of time before the scouts from nearby St Helens tempted him. He joined the Saints in August 1951, and his career with St Helens and Widnes, both of whom he led to Wembley Challenge Cup finals as captain in 1961 and 1964, proved the stepping stone to even higher honours with Great Britain, especially on the tour of Australia and New Zealand in 1958.

For a player whose name is held in awe Down Under, where parents were rumoured to have frightened their children into going to bed with the threat that 'Karalius is coming', it is amazing that of his 12 international caps only five were gained against the Australians. But what an impact he made in those five Tests, especially in the eventful second and third Tests of that successful 1958 tour. Vince's international career against the Australians would not have begun in 1958 but for the intervention of the manager, Mr Tom Mitchell. At the close of the meeting to select the 26-strong squad of players the name of Vince Karalius didn't figure on the list to be handed to the awaiting press corps. The alteration of the list to include the 6 feet, 14-stone 6-pound loose forward was due to the insistence of Mitchell, who reasoned that: 'I needed him to tame the likes of the Aussie hard men Norman Provan and Kel O'Shea. Karalius was just the big, strong, intimidating man for the job'. That Vince Karalius performed the job and earned the nickname 'The Wild Bull of the Pampas' for his rampaging runs and ferocious tackling is history. The Australians have never forgotten his deeds in that second Test when captain Alan Prescott broke his arm and Karalius had to operate in the stand off position. His attitude to Test rugby has served as an example to other aspiring Great Britain forwards.

Vince Karalius belonged to an era when loose forwards were expected to be creative footballers and ball distributors. He was the supreme No. 13 in these respects. Being a strong athletic player and extremely

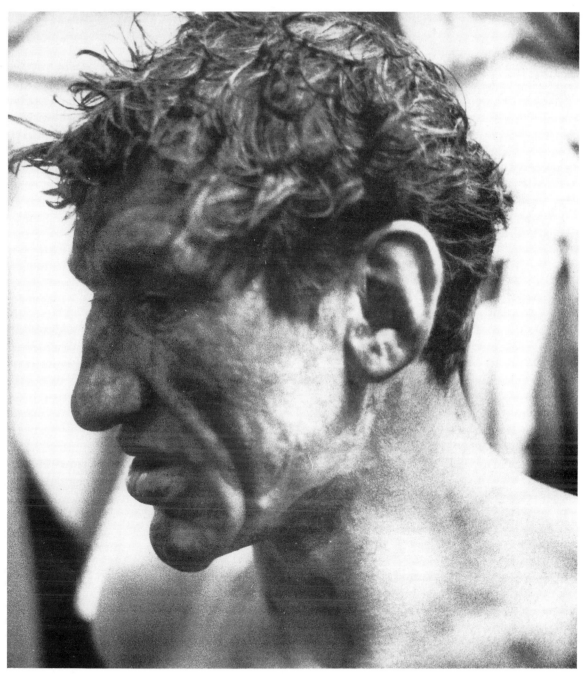

fit (he was reputed to have run from his house in Widnes to training at the St Helens ground, and then run back – a round trip of some 20 miles) he loved nothing better than to carry the ball. He had the ability to ride a tackle and stand upright in the attempted tackle before offloading the ball to a colleague in support. To perform this technique a forward needs immense upper body strength and pair of large, safe hands. Karalius had both and he put them to good effect in his tackling, too.

'Wild Bull' Vince Karalius, whose massive rugged face symbolised Rugby League.

117

He would leap onto his opponent, usually from a frontal position, and clamp his arms around the player almost like an octopus, squeezing the very lifeblood out of the player. Few passed him in an open field situation and scrum halves realised that a break down on the blind side of a scrum when Karalius faced them at loose forward could lead to the end of a promising career.

Vince's appetite for the sport could not be satisfied when he retired from playing and it was inevitable that he would find his way into coaching. His coaching spells at Wigan and Widnes were highly success-ful, and his insistence on personal fitness surely heralded the modern era of Rugby League, in which the level of fitness compares favourably with that of all other winter sports.

BRETT KENNY

I readily confess to the fact that the Australian centre or stand off Brett Kenny is one of the few players who has left me speechless during one of my B.B.C. Television commentaries. My shocked silence was not, however, caused by one of his superb match performances but occurred before the match had even kicked off. During the traditional naming of players and the subsequent peeling off from the team line-ups at Wembley for the 1985 Silk Cut Challenge Cup final, Brett Kenny stunned the crowd and, I should think, surprised the millions watching on television when, instead of running to his place on the field, he turned, hunched his shoulders and strolled nonchalantly back to Wigan's half of the pitch. His calm, cool, almost arrogant approach upset one or

b. 16.3.1961
Parramatta, Wigan,
Australia

Brett Kenny, the Kangaroos' gifted midfield player, gives a fine exhibition of his balanced running as he outmanoeuvres Great Britain's Deryck Fox.

two traditionalists in the crowd but all was forgiven when he was awarded the Lance Todd Trophy for his outstanding display in Wigan's win over Hull. As Brett Kenny later commented, his behaviour was all part of his preparation for the big game: 'I tried simply to detach myself from all of the hysteria. It's my normal way of preparing myself for the task ahead. If I offended anyone then it was unintentional'.

Such calmness, even studied casualness, is at the heart of Brett Kenny's success as a player, for in his 16 Tests he has displayed that ability to detach himself from the emotional atmosphere surrounding such matches to give a methodical, even clockwork, performance, especially when playing at stand off.

At almost 6 feet and 13 stones 'Bert', as he is known to all his friends in rugby, is not in the usual mould of Australian stand offs. Most of the Kangaroos' classy practitioners in the No. 6 jersey have been of the short, squat, physical type given to producing short, jinking, piercing runs to split a defence before handing on to even speedier centre threequarters. Players like Vic Hey, Bobby Fulton and Brian Clay spring to mind. Brett Kenny has a long stride and exceptional speed which enables him to complete many of his devastating breaks with tries, even when the opposition line is 60 or 70 yards distant. Of his 19 tries scored in only 25 appearances while guesting for the Wigan club in 1984–85 it is perhaps his never-to-be-forgotten try in the Cup final defeat of Hull that best illustrates his running skills. He exhibited balanced running at its best and a remarkable change of pace which took him around the luckless Hull full back Gary Kemble before he touched down at the end of his 70-yard tryscoring run.

In Australia he is best remembered for his service to the Parramatta club, whom he joined from Guildford in 1980. Since then he has helped them to five Sydney Grand Finals. Brett Kenny probably reached the greatest heights in his long list of achievements when, having displaced the vice captain, Wally Lewis, from the Australian No. 6 position, he proved the lynchpin of that magnificent unbeaten Kangaroo touring team of 1982. At 21 he was the youngest member of the touring party, yet he displayed a remarkable maturity and a nonchalance that remained undiminished when he returned to Wembley three years later. It was indeed a fitting honour to his talents when he was named the Adidas Golden Boot winner as the greatest League player in 1986. Although he was forced to miss the whole of the 1988 season Down Under on account of a serious knee ligament problem I sincerely hope that Brett recovers to silence me again, perhaps this time with one of his skilful match performances.

LEN KILLEEN

When St Helens won four trophies in that memorable 1965–66 season the names of Alex Murphy, Tom Van Vollenhoven and Tommy Bishop rolled off the tongues of the fans at regular intervals as matches were won by their brilliant individual feats. Yet the one player who was never accorded the same praise during that season was the points-scoring machine on the left wing, Len Killeen, a player with a unique talent for scoring tries or goals at the crucial time in the most important of matches. Some players suffer from nerves and others from a lack of confidence in their own ability, but few have the control and confidence when under intense pressure Len Killeen had.

b. 19.11.1938
St Helens, Balmain

As an ex-basketball player Len was naturally skilful with a ball in his hands and, being an import from South African Rugby Union accustomed to plenty of opportunities for running on hard grounds, he had plenty of pace. What more could a winger want? But Len had more, he was one of the most powerful and accurate kickers of a ball I have ever seen. Indeed, he was so accurate that he could have had a great career as the goalkicker with an American Pro Football team. For Rugby League's sake, thank goodness he turned down that opportunity. Although he played at St Helens for only five seasons, from 1962 to 1967, and did not have the chance to be the club goalkicker in his first two seasons, he collected 1,160 points from 115 tries and 408 goals. He topped the Rugby League points chart in three consecutive seasons between 1964 and 1967 and in season 1965–66 became the only player in the history of the game to finish at the top of all three charts, with figures of 32 tries, 120 goals and 336 points. But despite his appetite for points my memories of him will always be of his ability to snatch the vital match-winning try or goal when all seemed lost.

I'll never forget his interception try against Dewsbury in the 1966 Challenge Cup semi-final when the hot favourites, St Helens, were struggling with only 20 minutes of the match remaining. He caught the ball with perfect timing and sped 75 yards to score a try which set St Helens on the road to Wembley. And when he arrived at Wembley he crowned his Lance Todd Trophy-winning performance with one of the most incredible goals seen at the famous stadium. Amid intense pressure before a record attendance of 98,536, in the ninth minute of the match, when players' nerves are still in the settling stage, Len stepped up to display his uncanny coolness with a confidence-boosting penalty goal, surely the longest seen at Wembley. Placing the ball at a distance of 65 yards from the opposition goal posts and only eight yards in from the touchline he appeared to have little chance of gaining the two points. But the ball sailed firmly between the posts to set Saints on their way to a win over local rivals Wigan. His uncanny handling ability was also exhibited in that Cup final when, on chasing a grubber kick from his

centre Billy Benyon, he dived over and scooped up the ball for a try in one movement of his body and hands.

Len Killeen's feats on the field were often inspirational to others playing alongside him, for one of his vital goals or tries would often be the signal for his St Helens team to move into top gear and head for victory. Sadly for St Helens and British Rugby League fans, at the end of the 1966–67 season Len headed Down Under, where he was to experience considerable success with Balmain. Of course, he had little problem in establishing himself as their record goalkicker. In 1969 Len landed 84 goals as well as 6 drop goals and 9 tries for a total of 207 points, becoming the first Balmain player to top 200.

OPPOSITE: *St Helens' South African wing, Len Killeen, helps the author to quell an attack by the opposition.*

MAX KRILICH

b. 25.10.1950
Manly, Australia

In 1982 at Headingley, Leeds, after one of the finest ever exhibitions of Rugby League I've seen from any side, I was privileged to attend the after-match function in honour of the visiting Kangaroos. After their convincing 31–4 defeat of the pride of Yorkshire, I expected the Australian players to be in high spirits and ready to 'let their hair down'. Imagine the effect upon a wildly appreciative audience when Max Krilich, the skipper of the 1982 'Invincible' touring side, announced that he was fining two of his players for not wearing official blazers at the after-match reception. These were not the Aussies I used to know and love! Yet the disciplined and professional approach of the 32-year-old captain led to the emergence of one of the truly great teams in the history of world rugby, the 1982 Australian touring team, which roared through Britain and France winning all of their 22 matches. And they had much for which to thank this inspirational hooker in the manner in which he conducted their affairs both on and off the field.

Australian Test skipper Max Krilich acts as the ball-playing pivot against Great Britain in the 1982 Ashes series.

The hooking position is not normally one from which to lead a team, especially at international level, as the captain is usually a middle back or a full back. Such positions are away from the fiery exchanges and allow the captain a better view of how the play is developing around him. Surprisingly, Australia have fielded four Test captains in the

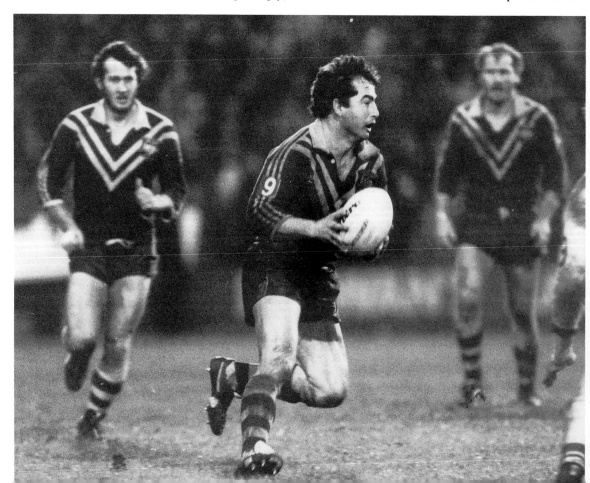

No. 9 role: Ken Kearney, Ian Walsh, George Peponis and Max Krilich himself. They have been well served by all of them, despite the critics' opinion that it is difficult to assess the pattern of a game when a player's head is buried in the scrum.

Max Krilich was a reliable rather than a brilliant ball-winner in the scrums, but his work around the play the balls (rucks) excelled that of all others. During the tour of 1982 he revived the art of running from the acting half back position and figured in many intricate moves with his forwards and backs. His quick, piercing runs and his passing of the ball to colleagues in close support devastated many a British defence. He created space out wide for his speedy backs by making sure that the opposition forwards remained in midfield to cover his opportunist breaks.

His 13 Test matches, coming rather late in his career, were a fitting reward for a player who served a long apprenticeship, tuning his skills, before emerging on the world Rugby League stage. Max made his debut for Manly, his only club in 15 years of rugby, at 20 years of age in 1969 in the Third Grade team, and played over 100 Reserve Grade matches before breaking into the First Grade. His Test debut came against New Zealand in 1978 when he was 28. Once he had made the breakthrough, he never looked back; he played a record 334 Grade games for Manly, 215 of which were First Grade. A model of consistency, Max Krilich was an example to all aspiring professional League players.

GRAEME LANGLANDS

b. 2.10.1941
St George, Australia

A recent editorial in Australia's highly respected *Rugby League Week* magazine about the Sydney City v Country Districts match, a traditional feature on the Australian Rugby League calendar for many years, observed coldly that, 'If there is any future for a Sydney v Country game of some sort, it lies in the bush where it will at least draw a reasonable crowd. The only excuses for its continuation, as I see it, are tradition and the chance for young country bucks to show their wares before eagle-eyed Sydney scouts, who probably know all there is to know about them anyway'. Indeed, the fixture now has difficulties in attracting the public's attention or the crowds. But if such games were not on the calendar many a country boy could be denied the centre stage necessary for him to force his way into the reckoning with the big Sydney clubs.

Australian Test rugby's most prolific points-scorer, Graeme Langlands, could have been such a player. He burst onto the scene after one spectacular performance for the Country team in 1962. Within a season the lad from Wollongong had represented New South Wales at full back and was on his way to a glorious career with the mighty St George club. Within another year he had made his debut at Test level against New Zealand in the centre and joined that select band of players who can boast of international caps against South Africa. From such humble origins began a great career and surely, if only to unearth other future Australian stars, the Sydney v Country match deserves to be continued.

Throughout his 34 international appearances Graeme Langlands had the ideal build, at 6 feet and 13 stones, to play in either the full back or centre positions. In every aspect of play he was a fierce competitor and at his best when the going was at its toughest. Yet he had the coolness and the self-assurance to become Australia's top points-scorer in Anglo/Australian Tests with 104 points to his credit. His total of 43 goals is the highest number recorded by any Australian player against Great Britain, while his individual tally of 20 points in a Test match stood as a joint record until Michael O'Connor erased Graeme's name from the record books in 1986 with 22 points. He is the only player to play in six Anglo/Australian series and only Sandy Pearce, the Easts forward who played for Australia for 13 years, has beaten his achievement of playing against Great Britain from 1963 to 1974. Graeme had the honour of captaining Australia in four Test matches but sadly, when he was captain-coach of the 1973 Kangaroo tour, a hand injury cost him at least another two occasions to be first to run onto the field in a green and gold jersey. 'Changa', as he was known, was equally at home at either centre or full back, happy to be out there on the field competing for St George or Australia.

OPPOSITE: *A supreme attacking full back, Graeme Langlands was never afraid to pressure opponents with one of his long punts upfield.*

JAMES LEULUAI

b. 4.2.1957
Ellerslie, Mt Wellington,
Hull, Leigh, Petone,
Wakefield Trinity, New
Zealand

During my career as the Rugby League commentator for B.B.C. Television I have had the pleasure of describing many outstanding tries, but few have equalled the two scored by Hull centre James Leuluai in the Silk Cut Challenge Cup final and the replay at Elland Road, Leeds in May 1982. For speed of execution, delivery of a sidestep and precision passing they took the breath away and highlighted all the qualities that enabled James to become a permanent fixture in the centre for New Zealand between 1979 and 1986.

His first try in that never-to-be-forgotten Wembley classic between Hull and Wigan saw him receive the ball 50 yards from the Wigan try line, straighten up, move off with a sudden burst of acceleration and, after two short, neat sidesteps, put the ball beneath the Wigan posts without anyone even touching him. His second, after a brilliant scissors movement with stand off David Topliss, illustrated his speed of thought, good handling ability and his timing in running onto a pass. Both tries were examples of how, in Rugby League back play, there is no substitute for speed.

That blistering pace of James Leuluai's was encouraged when, as a five-year-old in the town of Mangakino where he lived with his Samoan parents, he ran in the local athletics races over 50 yards. And dynamic pace over 50 yards is what is needed to split the tightest of midfield defences. He learned his early rugby too in Mangakino, with the juniors at Papatoetoe before leaving, aged 17, to join Ellerslie, where he played alongside his future Hull and Kiwi Test team-mate Gary Kemble. Having played for three seasons under the exciting coaching of Ken Stirling, he joined Mt Wellington and embarked on his successful New Zealand international career.

Speed was again the first priority of this classy centre when, at Mt Wellington and with the Kiwi Test squad, he came under the coaching influence of Cec Mountford, who insisted that he maintain his athletics track work. His speed, coupled with his other skills, enabled him to score the record number of tries for the New Zealand Test side – 24 in just 26 Tests. His opportunism and his performances when on tour in Great Britain with the Kiwis in 1980 attracted the attentions of Hull, who were about to rouse themselves out of a period of decline in the Second Division. James's signing, along with that of a trio of other Kiwis (Dane O'Hara, Fred Ah Kuoi and Gary Kemble), sparked off a great revival at Hull and produced a boom for Rugby League on Humberside.

The signing of overseas players by British clubs has often aroused considerable criticism, much of which has implied that much-needed finance is taken out of the country and that British youngsters are denied a chance to shine. James Leuluai and his fellow countrymen easily refute those arguments, for during their reign Hull has experienced its biggest attendances for decades, often averaging crowds of 14,000. The skills and attitudes of the four Kiwis did much to attract youngsters to the club and enhanced their game when playing alongside them. James Leuluai's self-discipline and gentlemanly approach to rugby helped him to become the perfect ambassador for his country and his club, both on and off the field.

OPPOSITE: *James Leuluai's speed off the mark threatened danger whenever he was in possession of the ball.*

WALLY LEWIS

b. 1.12.1959
Valleys, Wakefield Trinity,
Wynnum Manly, Brisbane
Broncos, Australia

Does Wally Lewis, for me Australia's greatest stand off and captain, ever move on a rugby pitch? Whenever I watch him he seems to be standing still, completely in the clear, spraying out a series of breathtakingly long passes or defence-splitting shorter passes to forwards in close support. He indulges in monstrous kicks to touch, short grubber kicks or high kicks up to the opposition full back. And, whenever he scores a try, he seems to stroll nonchalantly through the widest of gaps as if there is an embargo placed on anyone touching him. Yet such is

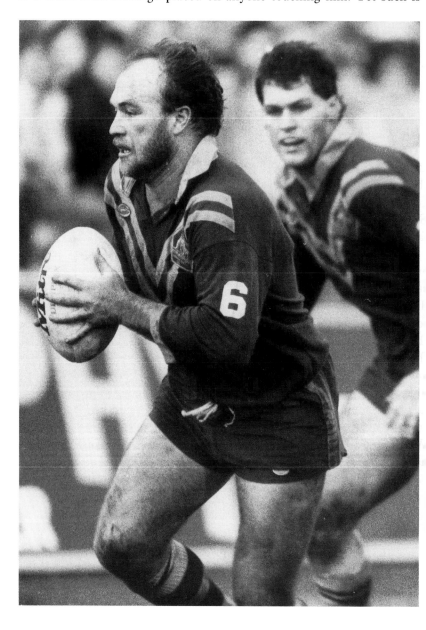

A perfect example of Wally Lewis's characteristic manner of holding the ball, well away from his body. It enables him to pass effectively and to switch direction to any side.

the class of this Queensland hero that he makes all the time and space in which to perform his full repertoire of tricks. Although often abused in the rival state of New South Wales, there is little doubt that Wally Lewis has been the conductor of Australia's dominance in Rugby League for the past few seasons, having orchestrated nearly every move of the team. As captain of his country in the Ashes series of 1984 and 1986 he has reigned supreme in his side's whitewash of Great Britain. Such talent is obviously God-given, but few appreciate the many hours of work and dedication needed to harness all the skills and refine them.

Like his great Australian counterpart in cricket, Don Bradman, who spent his youth in Bowral hitting a cricket ball against a tree with a bat, Wally spent his afternoons kicking a ball at a particular section of a wall or passing and bouncing the ball off any nearby object. In this way he perfected his passing and kicking skills. Having joined the Ella brothers on the famous Australian Schoolboys' Rugby Union tour which swept through the British Isles in 1977, Wally Lewis turned to his first love, Rugby League, and joined the junior section of the Valleys club in Brisbane in 1978. In 1984 he moved to the more wealthy Wynnum Manly club as captain-coach before he helped the Australian Rugby League to launch a truly national Premiership League by forming the Brisbane Broncos in 1988. Wally Lewis had always resisted the lure of the wealthier Sydney clubs but when Brisbane, along with the Gold Coast Giants and the Newcastle Knights, were included to expand the Sydney League competition, there was no doubt that Queensland's favourite son would captain Brisbane.

Often controversial and temperamental because of his strong attitudes and commanding presence on a field, he started a trend among Australian stars when he signed a lucrative short-term contract for Wakefield Trinity in 1983. Since then, many Australian players have bolstered the fortunes of English clubs and, likewise, English players have entertained the crowds in the Sydney and Brisbane competitions, but few have made the sensational impact of Wally Lewis. The mind boggled when it was announced that Trinity were to make Wally the first player in the history of the game to receive match payments of £1,000 per appearance. Many talked of exploitation, some predicted the code edging towards financial ruin but Trinity doubled their gates, recouped their financial outlay and Wally Lewis rewarded them with six tries in ten appearances. His move has done much to rejuvenate and enhance the British game.

JAMES LOMAS

b. 6.2.1882
Bramley, Salford, Oldham,
York, Great Britain

Cumbria is especially renowned as the home of good, strong forward rough-hewn out of the hills, and yet over the years the county has bee known to produce many an international back. Few more prominen players have emerged than James Lomas, the boy from Maryport, who prior to the First World War, became such a prolific points-scorer tha there were few records he did not achieve in his long career.

In season 1987–88, to accompany the new players' contract system a the clubs, the Rugby League's ruling body introduced an arbitratio. panel to settle any arguments on transfers of players between club outside the players' contractual period. It was hardly an innovation, a some thought: James Lomas, in his transfer from Bramley to Salford i 1901, barely a season after joining the Yorkshiremen from the amateu ranks of Maryport, was the subject of a similar arbitration panel. And when the deal was eventually settled to everyone's satisfaction, he becam the world's first £100 transfer. To be worth such a sum he had to b something special.

Players in Rugby League at the turn of the century were much smalle than they are today: the St Helens pack in the first ever Challenge Cup final of 1896 weighed in at barely 12 stones 6 pounds per man. Thus at 13 stones and 5 feet 7 inches, James Lomas was built like a pocke battleship and, blessed with a fair turn of speed, he was exceptionall difficult to tackle when he had built up his momentum. Being low t the ground, this nuggety centre could bustle opponents out of the wa and create the gaps to enable him to score his frequent tries. His strengt and squat build were also an asset in his special skill of goalkicking.

His points-scoring feats are all the more remarkable if we conside that in his playing days there were fewer opportunities then for a kic at goal and, with 15 men in each team until the beginning of seaso 1906–07, there were more opponents to beat before a try could be score Yet some of his records still stand today. James Lomas's individual tall of 39 points in a match for Salford v Liverpool City in 1907 is still th club record, while only David Watkins and Gus Risman have sinc scored more points for Salford than the 1,570 accumulated by Lomas In his first season he amply illustrated why Salford had paid £100 fo his services when he collected 266 points for himself out of the club' total of 280 for the whole season. Some performance! Naturally, whe he returned home in 1910 after captaining the first Northern Union tou abroad, during which he scored 10 tries and 53 goals in 13 matche Down Under, he was much in demand – so much so that Oldham agree to break the transfer record yet again, paying £300 for his services fo the next four seasons. He retired in 1915 after a brief spell with York

In my own playing era, the 1960s, it was not uncommon for a playe to continue in Rugby League until he was about 34 years of age. Today

*James Lomas' individual
tally of 39 points in a match,
achieved against Liverpool
City in 1907, remains a club
record over 80 years later.*

with the greater emphasis on speed and the more regular internation
competition, players tend to retire very soon after they reach 30. I
Australia, where the harder grounds take their toll, the players ofte
retire from First Grade rugby at 28. James Lomas had such an appetit
for the game, as well as great stamina and fitness, that in 1923, eigh
years after his retirement, he returned to help Salford for eight match
at the great age of 41.

JOE LYDON

Wembley Stadium on Challenge Cup final day has proved to be the perfect setting for Joe Lydon, Wigan's pacy midfield back, to display his full range of talents. From his first appearance there, playing for Wigan Schools Under 11s in the junior curtain-raiser prior to the showpiece final, to his latest encounter with Halifax in 1988, he has always risen to the occasion. His thrilling 70-yard, curving run from full back to set up a try for Wigan loose forward Ellery Hanley in that Cup final victory over Halifax and his two long distance tries for Widnes against Wigan in the final of 1984 proved once again that there is no substitute for speed. And Joe Lydon has that in abundance.

b. 26.11.1963
Widnes, Wigan, Eastern Suburbs, Great Britain

Speedy threequarter Joe Lydon is just too late to escape the clutches of Wally Lewis in Wigan's match against the Kangaroos in 1986.

At 6 feet 1 inch and 13 stones, Joe moves gracefully upfield, seemingly able to beat the most ferocious tacklers with an outside swerve or a feint to the left or right. His try in the first Test against Australia at Old Trafford in 1986, which won him the prize of top television try of the season, highlighted all those qualities and gave proof of what a beautifully balanced runner he is. Whether operating at full back, wing or centre Joe is most dangerous when given half a chance to run in space, especially at full back, where his line kicking ranks with the best today. He is able to use the room afforded when fielding a kick deep in his own half to launch devastating counterattacks. On the wing, when given an overlap he is a lethal finisher and could surely have been a great Test winger if he had continued in that role after his international debut for Great Britain, when he scored a try against France at Carcassonne in 1983 as a 19-year-old novice.

Joe, like Shaun Edwards and Mick Burke (two other Great Britain internationals), benefited from playing both codes of rugby as a schoolboy, thanks to the breakdown in recent years of the hostility between the two codes and the growth of comprehensive schools. In the North of England in particular Rugby Union was the preserve of the grammar school while the secondary modern school practised the League code. The mergers between the two systems and the resultant comprehensive schools and sixth form colleges afforded youngsters unprecedented opportunities to play League. Hence schoolboys now become dual internationals at both League and Union. While playing Rugby League with the St Patrick's amateur League youth side and John Rigby High School, Joe Lydon also represented Lancashire and England Schools on their Union tour of Zimbabwe in 1982, thus achieving distinction at both codes.

A player of Joe Lydon's quality, with the ability to score tries from long range positions on the field, will always be in demand and it is significant that the two most consistent cup-winning sides of the 1980s, Widnes and Wigan (who bought him for a world record fee of £100,000 in season 1985–86), have commanded his services. Eastern Suburbs, Sydney also availed themselves of his many talents during a summer stint in 1987. Now a qualified graphic designer, he will no doubt weave intricate patterns on the field of play for many seasons to come.

STAN McCORMICK

When Stan McCormick coached me in my early years in League at St Helens his players rarely lacked team spirit, for his ready wit and infectious humour enlivened many a training session. He was an entertainer who treated the players as his audience. In his own playing days from 1945 to 1954 he captivated and entertained the crowds with his distinctive brand of wing-play, to which he added a touch of daring that often made them hold their breath in anticipation of his antics.

Stan's sidestepping thrilled the fans wherever he played; while his

b. 5.7.1922
Belle Vue Rangers,
St Helens, Warrington,
Great Britain

137

PREVIOUS PAGE: *Great Britain's second Test against Australia in 1948. Stan McCormick, the great entertainer, shakes hands with the Hon. J. M. Tully.*

runs across field, from which he often scored on his opposite wing, upset the tightest of defences. Having played at scrum half in his Lancashire Schoolboys days, he liked nothing better than to leave his wing and scamper in midfield to open up a gap for his team-mate on the other wing. Many of the great Brian Bevan's tries were started by one of Stan McCormick's probing runs during his spell at Warrington. He also had pace, that most vital of assets for any wingman, and took special care to see that he never lost the instant acceleration off the mark that was his key to success. In the immediate post-War years Stan used to take part with other speed merchants from Rugby League like Brian Bevan and Griff Jenkins, in numerous professional sprint races held in the North of England. And he had considerable success too, as his victory in the Empire Open Sprint Handicap at Halifax in 1948, a competition open to all professional runners, indicates.

His speciality was the interception try, a feat which when performed well, is applauded; but when the interception is missed, it can lead to a try against the player attempting it and hoots of derision from the crowd. Perfect timing is the key to an interception try and Stan insists, jokingly, that he learned this while playing for Belle Vue Rangers when the team were in desperate straits. Despite fielding Test players of the calibre of Ray Price, Elwyn Gwyther, Doug Phillips and Stan himself, the team were usually close to the bottom of the league with the result that, as Stan says: 'We rarely had the ball and the only way we could get the ball was for me to attempt an interception. I scored from 16 interceptions in the 1947–48 season'. Whatever his reasons, his skill in the act was incomparable.

Such were his talents that it was obvious that Belle Vue Rangers would be unable to retain him for long and it was no surprise when he was transferred to St Helens in 1948, the year of his three Test appearances against Australia, for a world record fee of £4,000. Although he won an array of medals with St Helens he was forced to wait until he transferred to Warrington before he was able to collect a Challenge Cup winner's medal. But that medal, in 1954, was well worth collecting as it was won on one of the most memorable occasions in Rugby League's history; the replay with Halifax at Odsal, Bradford attracted a world record crowd of 102,575. It was a wonderful finale to the career of a player whose sole aim on the rugby pitch was to entertain as many people as he could.

TOMMY McCUE

In the small northern towns of Widnes, Leigh or Warrington Rugby League players can attain a status akin to that often reserved for film stars or pop stars in the capitals of the world. Just to catch sight of them gives many youngsters the same thrill as waiting outside stage doors for a glimpse of the famous does for others. Frank Tobin, the long-serving Widnes club physiotherapist who has seen every great player to wear the black and white colours of this friendly Cheshire club over the past 50 years, bears testimony to the greatness and impact of the Great Britain scrum half Tommy McCue. He recalls how he once rushed home as a youngster to inform his father, 'I've seen Tommy McCue in the street today'. And he reveals how, after Widnes' 1934 first round Cup defeat of a Leeds team containing 11 internationals, the Leeds Chairman put a blank cheque on the committee room table and asked the Widnes Chairman to fill it in for McCue's transfer to the Yorkshire club. Thankfully for the 'Chemics', as Widnes are known, he was not foolish enough to put pen to paper.

A local boy from St Bede's School, a nursery of many fine Widnes players, Tommy McCue at 5 feet 8 inches and 13 stones was blessed with the one virtue that all scrum halves yearn to possess – speed. His phenomenal pace was responsible for breaking down many a tight defence, especially when he chose to scurry away from the scrum down the blind side in the opposition's 25-yard area. His links with the loose forward and his club stand off partner, Tom Shannon, were timed to perfection, often resulting in a try for a colleague in support.

Not a prolific tryscorer himself – he scored only three tries on the 1936 tour Down Under and was the only player who failed to score on the 1946 tour – he was a creator of play and a shrewd judge when kicking the ball. He was one of that rare breed of player who is able to detach himself from the hurly-burly of the match to look at the tactics being employed and, with great vision, to change the direction of attack if need be. On that 1946 tour only Tommy McCue and Gus Risman had played Test rugby before, and Tommy's experience was a vital factor in the Ashes victory, especially his astute half back play with Willie Horne, the Barrow stand off. Nor did he forget his tactical kicking for, in the second Test which Great Britain won 14–5, a shrewd kick led to one of Arthur Bassett's tries, his second coming after a switch move by McCue down the blind side.

But Tommy McCue was essentially a Widnes lad and his greatest thrill was to lead this unfashionable club to victories over the glamour teams of the era. His side's 7–3 defeat of Wigan in the Lancashire Cup final of 1945, after they had trailed until the 73rd minute, gave him his greatest moment at Naughton Park. 'My team was on the defensive for practically the whole of the game', he recalled. 'At last we got a footing

b. 23.9.1913
Widnes, Great Britain

Tactical genius Tommy McCue pictured at the Sydney Cricket Ground, the scene of many of his most famous Test triumphs.

in their 25-yard area. I put a short kick directly under the posts from the scrum and Reynolds made no mistake about scoring. I captained them to the first Lancashire Cup win in the club's history.'

BRIAN McTIGUE

Brian McTigue's two greatest attributes in Rugby League were, in fact, developed in basketball and boxing, which occupied the earlier part of his sporting life. The skills and mental toughness that he learned in those two sports were put to good use in the Wigan and Great Britain colours as he destroyed many an opponent with his ingenious ball control or with his strength and ferocity in the tackle or the scrum. As a physical training instructor with the Royal Artillery during his compulsory two years' National Service, Brian developed a liking for basketball. Indeed, while stationed in Ireland, he was good enough to be selected for the Ulster team. Quick handling, speed of passing and an ability to change the direction of attack instinctively were all skills which he brought to Rugby League, but they had been fashioned with a basketball in the gymnasium. He always recommended basketball to any aspiring young-ster as the ideal training for Rugby League. 'It is the best game for a forward to play', he said. 'Passes are thrown at you from all angles, at all heights, and at great speed to beat the opposition's close marking.'

b. 8.8.1930
Wigan, Bathurst, Great
Britain

Such was the sporting background that created his superb ball-handling ability, never better illustrated for myself and St Helens than on one fateful day in February 1965 when one pass of his, timed to the split-second, knocked us out of the second round of the Challenge Cup 7–2. Amid a sea of mud and driving rain both teams were locked in a titanic forward battle until Brian slipped a short pass out of the tackle to his pack colleague Roy Evans, who raced under the posts for the winning try. The pass was the trademark of a master ball-playing prop: it travelled barely a foot and moved through a gap barely a foot wide.

His strength as a prop forward and his toughness in the tackle were surely developed in his other sporting love, boxing. He had featured in over 50 professional fights before taking up Rugby League and so was already steeled for the task when he made his debut for Wigan in 1951. That debut, and his signing for the famous Lancashire club, came only after he had been persuaded to try his hand at Rugby League for the Giants Hall colliery team when they were a man short. Thank goodness a regular did not turn up, for once Brian McTigue had learned the rudiments of the game over the next couple of seasons in Wigan's Alliance League team, he was to grace the town team and his country with his unparalleled skills.

Although Brian was, both on and off the pitch, a very quiet, modest and amiable man, his League record speaks volumes for his ability. In six Challenge Cup final appearances with Wigan at Wembley he gained three winner's medals and was awarded the Lance Todd Trophy for his display in the 30–13 Cup final defeat of Hull in 1959. With Wigan, his only club in Britain, he gained every honour the game has to offer, including 25 caps. He visited Australia and New Zealand on two very

Brian McTigue.

141

successful Great Britain tours in 1958 and 1962 before his departure to join Bathurst in New South Wales. However, his career in Australia was somewhat short-lived and it was not long before he returned to Wigan, as he preferred, I think, the quieter comforts of a simple Lancashire life to the more pacy lifestyle of Australia. Sadly Brian died at the age of 51 in 1981 and Great Britain lost one of its finest rugby ambassadors, a man who remained modest to the end and allowed his deeds to speak for him.

OPPOSITE: *Wigan and Great Britain prop Brian McTigue, who was best known as a creator of tries, records a well-deserved try of his own in Wigan's 1959 Challenge Cup final win against Hull.*

143

MAL MENINGA

b. 8.7.1960
Souths Brisbane, St Helens,
Canberra, Australia

To this day Joe Warham, the Company Secretary of the Leeds Rugby League Club, never ceases to quiz me as to how, in the summer of 1984, I managed to beat him to the signature of Mal Meninga, the giant centre from Souths, Brisbane. If I was of a boastful nature I would proclaim that good judgement and clever persuasion gave me the edge when securing his services for my old club, St Helens. But, being honest, I would admit that it was due more to good luck and making sure that I was in the right place at the right time and one step ahead of Joe and his Chairman, Harry Jepson. There was certainly no more relieved man in Australia than me when, ten minutes after the final whistle of the second Test at Lang Park, Brisbane, I secured Mal Meninga's signature on a one-season playing contract for St Helens while standing in the corridor outside the victorious Kangaroos' dressing room. It was a costly signing for St Helens but, when one considers that we were buying a 6 feet, 16-stone, points-scoring machine, Mal was a bargain.

Of the 28 tries he scored in 31 matches for the Saints in season 1984–85, two against Hull Kingston Rovers in the end-of-season Premiership final indicated the all-round talents of this modest player. He was a gentle giant on the field but when roused he was devastating; his tackle on the big Rovers centre, Gary Prohm, sent a shudder around the terraces, such was the bodily contact and crunch of the impact. His defence was impeccable. His monstrous hand-off, a tactic so rarely used these days by modern centres, can send a defender reeling and several Rovers players felt its full force in their faces as he ran for his first try in that Premiership final at Elland Road, Leeds. His second try, for which he outpaced the Great Britain wing, Gary Clark, showed his phenomenal speed for such a big man. Once he had broken the cover there was no catching 'Mighty Mal'.

Mal's achievements on the Kangaroo tour of Europe in 1982, during which he scored a record 48 points in a Test series in England and collected 118 points on the whole trip from 50 goals and six tries in just ten appearances, are a tribute to those skills. But I think his finest attributes are his handling and passing ability, unusual in such a big player. Mal has huge hands, yet the ball passes through them with great delicacy and, even in the tightest situations, he is able to time his passes to his wing partner to perfection. On top of this, his positional sense is uncanny.

Few people will argue on the field with this ex-policeman who started his career with a police academy team in Queensland under the coaching of Wayne Bennett and continued under the same coach at Souths before joining Canberra in 1986 to link up once more with his mentor. Sadly, two serious breaks to his arm necessitated the insertion of a steel plate along the bone, which severely disrupted a career that was about to come

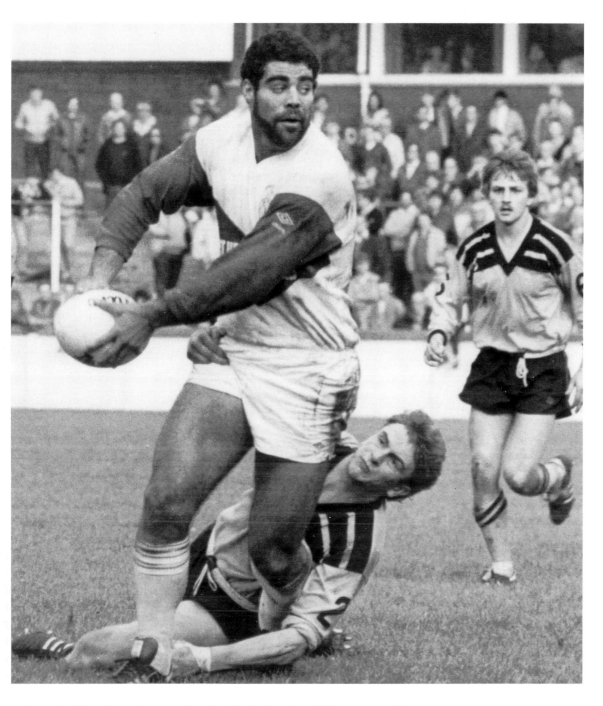

to its peak. Happily, after months of quiet dedication, Mal overcame his injury problem. He returned to the Test scene with Australia in 1988 only to lose another lucrative contract with St Helens when he suffered a further break to his arm.

As well as scoring 28 tries for St Helens in 1984–85, giant Australian centre Mal Meninga created many more through his skilful passing.

HERBERT 'DALLY' MESSENGER

b. 12.4.1883
Eastern Suburbs, Australia

There is little doubt that, without the presence of 'Dally' Messenger in the first ever game of Rugby League staged in Australia, the new rival code to Union would have struggled to gain the attention of the sporting public of Sydney. His appearance in that first match, Australia v New Zealand on 17th August 1907, not only guaranteed a 20,000 crowd at the Agricultural Showground but helped to found what is now the premier winter sport of the states of New South Wales and Queensland.

When Victor Trumper, the famous Australian Test cricketer, and James Giltinan, a local businessman, attempted to help a Rugby Union player, Alec Burdon, receive some recompense for a serious collar bone injury in 1907, their plans soon led them towards the idea of payments for players, rather in the manner of the sums of money then being given to Northern Union players in the breakaway leagues in Great Britain. The arrival of a New Zealand touring team, led by Mr A. H. Baskerville, on its way to compete in Britain under the new League rules gave them the opportunity to launch the rival code in Sydney. Many Union players who had suffered severe loss of wages through injury rallied to Giltinan's idea of a professional Australian team to tackle the 'All Golds', as the New Zealanders were known.

Both entrepreneurs knew that they needed a star personality to capture the imagination of the crowds if the venture was to succeed and they were convinced that Dally Messenger, the pride of Double Bay, was the man. As a small boy Herbert Messenger had been nicknamed 'Dally' by his father because he looked like the Premier of New South Wales, William Dalley. He was the toast of Australian Rugby Union: he was captain of Eastern Suburbs and had led New South Wales against the famed All Blacks in 1906. It took Trumper and Giltinan the whole evening of the 16th, not to convince Dally Messenger to play in three matches against the All Golds for a sum of £180, but to persuade his mother, Annie, to let him sign. She finally relented and thus Rugby League in Australia began.

Messenger's impact on the fledgling code was immense. He was taken along with the New Zealanders on that first trip to Britain in 1907–08 as a special attraction, he captained Australia in two Tests on their first tour in 1908–09 and skippered his nation for the first Test of the first Ashes series on home soil in 1910. Wherever he played he drew the crowds, and nowhere was this Eastern Suburbs League player more popular than in England. This is shown by the fact that when the Australians' tour ran into financial trouble a sign was put up outside the grounds, in an attempt to encourage spectators, which read: 'Messenger is playing today'.

He was a fine runner with the ball and a centre who liked to roam in midfield looking for the gaps, while his passing and handling was of the

Without 'Dally' Messenger's contribution to the first-ever Rugby League game in Australia, against New Zealand in 1907, the infant code might never have prospered there.

highest order. When wet weather made the ball slippery he would wear a jersey impregnated at the front with powdered resin and would rub his hands and the ball on it. I can remember the Great Britain Test prop Alan Prescott using a similar device in his playing days 50 years later. His skill as a goalkicker and his agility on his feet, which enabled him to avoid the most deadly of tacklers, attracted the soccer scouts when he was on tour in England and he was offered £1,500 to play soccer for Tottenham Hotspur in London. Thankfully, for the good of Australian Rugby League, he declined the offer.

Dally bore the weight and future success of Australian Rugby League on his shoulders with ease in those early, pioneer days. He was always the star attraction on the field, his tryscoring ability ensuring that the crowds flocked to support the new venture. A local sportswriter, 'Forward', reports his ability to score in the second Test of that 1909 Australian tour: 'Messenger was the hero, securing the ball in midfield, the Australian captain dodged, swerved and beat man after man. It seemed an impossible feat for him to get through, but player after player fell in attempting to tackle him and Messenger finished a glorious exhibition by placing the ball between the goalposts'.

There is no better tribute to Dally Messenger's place in the history of Australian Rugby League than the picture of him in the maroon and blue jersey of the Kangaroo tour of 1908–09 that adorns the foyer of the Sydney League's club. There is no name inscribed below, it is merely captioned 'The Master'.

ROGER MILLWARD

Anyone who suffers a succession of broken jaws, lasts 16 seasons in the hard world of professional Rugby League and is only 5 feet 4 inches and 10 stones 10 pounds must surely have something special – Roger 'the Dodger' Millward certainly did. From his schooldays, when he used to entertain millions on Sunday afternoons when I.T.V. transmitted amateur rugby matches, his ability to sidestep and jink his way through the tightest defences, his shrewd distribution of the ball, his tactical kicking and his sheer courage were there for all to see. He quickly attracted the professional clubs' talent scouts who joined the regular viewers in ever increasing numbers. But, as his school was only a few yards from the Wheldon Road ground at Castleford, it was only natural that his home town club should tempt him to sign professional forms and to give him the chance to make his debut against Dewsbury in October 1963.

b. 16.9.1947
Castleford, Hull Kingston Rovers, Cronulla, Great Britain

Roger 'The Dodger' Millward was adept at weaving his way through the tightest of defences.

Sadly for 'Classy Cas', as his home town team are known, the path of this eager young star was blocked by one of the game's greatest ever half back partnerships, Alan Hardisty and Keith Hepworth, and it was obvious that his ambitions would lead him elsewhere. His move to Hull Kingston Rovers for a fee of £6,000 coincided with a great era for Rovers. Roger Millward played his part in this, not only as a player but also, in the 1980s, as a most knowledgeable coach.

My first sight of Roger was in the B.B.C. Television Floodlit final of 1965 when Castleford beat St Helens 4–0. I could scarcely comprehend how such a small youngster could compete against huge men. But, after 80 minutes, I soon learned that he possessed considerable pace, a keen eye for a gap and a strong tackle which belied his small frame. When I toured Australia with him during the 1968 World Cup I came to appreciate his shrewd rugby brain and the composure which he brought to half back play. He was always so calm and assured under pressure, and so relaxed in his approach to a match, however important it might be. It is little wonder that he developed into one of Rugby League's star attractions in the 1970s.

Roger Millward was a prolific points-scorer for Hull Kingston Rovers and became the code's top tryscorer with 38 in 1967–68, then a record for any stand off. In the second Test match against Australia in 1970, while adding to his 29 international caps, he equalled Lewis Jones' record of 20 points in a single Test match (two tries and seven goals) to help Great Britain to win 28–7.

Throughout the 1970s Roger became one of only seven men in the history of the game to play in five Anglo/Australian Test series. After the all-Humberside final between Hull and Hull Kingston Rovers in 1980 he retired and moved into coaching. So successful was he that every trophy on offer found its way into the Hull Kingston Rovers show cabinet. Quite rightly Roger brought honour to the Rugby League code and to himself when he was awarded the M.B.E. for a career during which he was noted not only for his ability but especially for his sportsmanship.

CEC MOUNTFORD

b. 16.6.1919
Blackball, Wigan

The coal mines in and around Wigan have produced many international players, not only for the world famous club, but also for others close by in Lancashire. Cec Mountford, the diminutive, stocky stand off from Blackball, New Zealand, travelled 12,000 miles because of them. When overtures were made to Cec Mountford to play Rugby League in Britain it was natural that, being a student mining engineer, he should join an area with a rich mining background such as Wigan. The lad who had scored 67 goals and 31 tries in his final season with Blackball Rugby League Club helped to continue Wigan's tradition of fielding some of the finest stand offs in the world. After his arrival in England in July 1946, Cec extended his initial three-year contract to five years and delighted the Central Park faithful with his creative talent. At 5 feet 7 inches and 11 stones 7 pounds this half back was built like one of the nuggets of coal he had hewn out of the ground and soon forged a formidable partnership with Wigan local, Tommy Bradshaw, himself a player of great skill.

Cec's 17 tries in his first season were a prelude to better things and a foretaste of the skills he possessed. Few players had his ability to set a back line moving at top pace with swift and accurate passing, always delivered when on the move. Centres playing outside him could run onto the ball with perfect timing, such was the precision of his passing. His speed off the mark was phenomenal and he loved to slide through a defence which had moved up too quickly or which had left a gap wide enough for him to dash through. Once through he was rarely caught, as he took the ball in the direction of the outside centre and wing for the classic try at the corner flag.

He was not only a brilliant individual, but also a talented leader whose qualities were illustrated in his two most memorable matches and later in his successful coaching career. The Challenge Cup final of 1951 between Wigan and Barrow set the stage for Cec Mountford to become the first Wigan player, and the first Kiwi, ever to win the Lance Todd Trophy. His generalship at half back, his distribution and his defence-splitting bursts proved a problem for Barrow, especially for his opposite number, Willie Horne. His performance for Wigan in the Championship final of 1950, when the Lancashire side defeated the mighty Huddersfield despite the absence of eight internationals on tour, was the highlight of his playing career. From the second minute of the match, when he put emergency wing Nat Silcock in for a try, to the final whistle he gave an example of captaincy and stand off play that rarely has been bettered.

His sad departure from Wigan in 1951 to join Warrington on a ten-year coaching contract, surely one of the longest in modern times, allowed Cec to harness all the skills learned on the field of play and gave him the opportunity to encourage others to reach new peaks. Following

Cec Mountford, Wigan's brilliant Kiwi stand off, launches his threequarter line into the attack as two desperate Halifax defenders tear acrossfield to cover the movement.

his service to Warrington, he returned home to look after the coaching of the New Zealand international squads. The rise to prominence in the 1980s of the Kiwi sides and their magnificent Test defeats of Australia and Great Britain can be traced back to the earlier coaching work of Cec Mountford. New Zealand stars James Leuluai, Dane O'Hara, Fred Ah Kuoi and their colleagues owe so much to this little rugby maestro from Blackball, near Greymouth.

ALEX MURPHY

Alex Murphy was the most complete footballer I have ever seen in either code of rugby. Nor am I alone in holding that opinion, for the Rugby League scouts camped outside his parents' house days before his 16th birthday, awaiting the stroke of midnight after which they would be able to sign the schoolboy sensation. St Helens, for the somewhat derisory sum of £80, secured the signature of the scrum half who was to entertain millions throughout the world with his tricks, and torment every international side he played against. By the age of 19 he had established himself as the world's best scrum half, taking the crown from Australia's experienced Keith Holman in a series of fiery clashes in Australia during the 1958 Great Britain tour. It was then that he revealed his phenomenal pace as he scored 21 tries in only 20 outings.

His pace and his complete self-confidence were, for me, his greatest assets, although to pass no comment on his ability to sidestep, swerve, kick, tackle and pass would do him less than justice. He was unique in my playing and watching experience. The legendary Jim Sullivan was coach at St Helens when Alex first arrived at Knowsley Road and it was he who sharpened Alex's natural speed. He did not allow the precocious youngster to join in the usual games of touch rugby with the other players. Instead, he had to 'sprint, sprint, and sprint again between two pieces of silver paper placed on the cinder track at the front of the Saints' ground'. But how that discipline paid off! I well remember playing against Swinton in a Lancashire Cup match in which Alex, playing at scrum half, put the ball in the scrum, picked it up from behind my feet and scored beneath the posts from a distance of 25 yards before I could detach myself from the scrum. Some pace!

He had the supreme confidence and that touch of arrogance in his ability that enabled him to tower above his opponents and gave him a psychological advantage. He was never short of an answer, as was shown when one of his tries for St Helens in the third round of the Challenge Cup against Hull Kingston Rovers in 1966 proved more than controversial. His last-minute try scored beneath the posts, which helped us on our way to Wembley, was subject to consultations between referee Eric Clay and the touch judge before it was allowed. I too had grave doubts about the try, but not Alex. On being accosted by Rovers' fierce forward, Frank Foster, who disputed the try in no uncertain terms, he merely replied: 'Read the *Liverpool Echo* tomorrow night, Frank, and you'll see if it was a try!'

That confidence, after a ten-year playing career with St Helens which saw him appear twice at Wembley and gain 26 international caps (he was awarded one more at Warrington in 1971), helped Alex to become the most outspoken yet most successful coach in the history of Rugby League. In coaching spells at Leigh, Warrington, Wigan and St Helens

b. 24.4.1939
St Helens, Leigh,
Warrington, Great Britain

Alex Murphy.

153

*The phenomenal Alex
Murphy was the most
complete footballer I have
ever seen in either code of
rugby.*

he has taken all of them to Challenge Cup finals and won every trophy and honour available. His greatest feat was leading rank outsiders Leigh to a 24–7 victory over odds-on favourites Leeds in the 1971 final. Although his rugby knowledge is vast and his tactical appreciation is sounder than that of most coaches, it is as a motivator that he reigns supreme. His ability to pick a team off the dressing room floor at half time with a lashing from his tongue is legendary and yet 'Murphy the Mouth', as he is known in his weekly newspaper column, has a shrewd rugby brain.

It is interesting to reflect how some of the greatest of players in each code of rugby, League and Union, would have performed in the other. For some the arguments will always be hypothetical, but for Alex Murphy I have no doubt that his talents in Union, which he played when he was in the R.A.F. during his National Service, were second to none. Although he was once threatened by his station officer with being posted to Guam, a remote island in the Pacific, if he did not turn out on a Wednesday for the R.A.F. Union side, he proved equally adept in the rival code. Indeed, when playing once against Cambridge University at stand off he raced past the current England Union stand off, Richard Sharp, for three tries – a performance which earned the highest praise from Pat Marshall, the Rugby Union correspondent of the *Daily Express*: 'One of the truly great players of our time'. Yes, Alex Murphy certainly was that, at either code.

MICHAEL O'CONNOR

b. 30.11.1960
St George, Manly,
St Helens, Australia

Since the breakaway by the Northern Union from the Rugby Union in 1895 over 216 Rugby Union internationals to date have deserted the Union code in favour of the 13-a-side game in Great Britain. In Australia, especially in the states of New South Wales and Queensland, the number of converts is much smaller, since the code of Rugby Union is very much the lesser of the two rival rugby codes and its infiltration of schools tends to be in the grammar and independent sector. Hence the Union code provides many fewer converts than in the British Isles. But the Australian Rugby Union team does produce top quality players and when they are available the wealthy Sydney clubs are prepared to bid for their services. In the past, players like Ken Kearney, John Brass, Russell Fairfax and Phil Hawthorne have successfully made the transition from Union to League and, in more recent times, players of the calibre of Matt Burke and Brett Papworth have joined the League ranks. However, none has attained the prominence and respect of the Manly centre or wing, Michael O'Connor, whose rise to stardom since signing from Union in 1983 has been little short of meteoric.

His form in 13 Wallaby Union Tests had been duly noted by the Rugby League scouts and St George were the club to take the classy threequarter from the Teachers Rugby Union Club in Brisbane in 1983. Speed is a priceless asset in any player attempting to play in the threequarter line, while size is another invaluable weapon. If, like 13-stone Michael O'Connor, you happen to have both then you can be a winner. St George have had a habit of exploring the Rugby Union market and nurturing players into the League code – their ex-skipper Ken Kearney is a notable example. This they did with O'Connor before he surprised the Australian public by moving across Sydney to Manly at the beginning of the 1987 season. The Sea Eagles teamed him up with his old Wallaby colleague, Matt Burke, and by the 1988 season they presented a formidable attacking threat.

Michael O'Connor's goalkicking – he uses the round-the-corner style – would be enough to qualify him for any Hall of Fame, even after such a short League career. His deeds on his first tour abroad, within only two seasons of his move from Union, were to give notice of record-breaking feats to come. A tally of 3 tries and 13 goals from only four appearances on the tour of New Zealand in 1985 set the standard for this prolific points-scorer. His displays on the Kangaroos' tour of Great Britain and France put his name in the record books. A packed crowd of 50,000 at Old Trafford for the first Test of the series saw him smash the individual points tally for an Anglo/Australian Test match. For so long in a Test match the magical figure of 20 points had seemed to be unbeatable. Lewis Jones and Roger Millward of Great Britain and Graeme Langlands and Mick Cronin of Australia were all joint holders

The sensational Michael O'Connor, an ex-Wallaby Union player who has become a great favourite with the crowds Down Under.

of the individual points record, which had stood for some 32 years after Lewis Jones first achieved the mark in 1954. Along came Michael O'Connor who, in an almost casual manner, produced a hat trick of tries and five goals to score 22 points and to secure the record firmly for himself. With many more seasons to play, I feel sure that this sensational ex-Wallaby convert will re-write a few more records in his newly adopted code.

JONATHAN PARKIN

b. 5.11.1897
Wakefield Trinity, Hull
Kingston Rovers, Great
Britain

Occasionally a player comes along whose impact on the game is such that even the very rules are changed to accommodate him. Very often it seems to be fiery scrum halves who cause our legislators to think again. Such a player was Jonty Parkin, the Wakefield Trinity and Great Britain scrum half, whose transfer to Hull Kingston Rovers in 1930 caused a furore. Having signed for Wakefield Trinity at 15 years of age on 12th March 1913, the young Parkin pocketed the sum of £5.00, for which he gave 17 years of service to Trinity. After those 17 years he was placed on the transfer list, despite one contemporary comment that 'Wakefield without Parkin is like *Hamlet* without the Prince'. However, Wakefield were reluctant to let him go and so set his fee at £100 – very high for someone near the end of his career. Parkin responded by paying the fee himself and declared that he was now a free agent. He quickly signed for Hull Kingston Rovers, leaving the Trinity committee amazed at his cheeky initiative. He played for Rovers for only one season, but his actions caused the Rugby League's ruling body to change the rules so that in future no individual could pay his own transfer fee.

Great Britain skipper Jonty
Parkin and his squad return
home in triumph after the
1928 tour of Australia
aboard the Duchess of
Atholl.

Jonty Parkin was something special in an era of great half backs. As a young pit worker in the tiny Yorkshire mining village of Sharlston he displayed the exceptional talent on the games field which was to take him on three Great Britain tours in 1920, 1924 and 1928. He had considerable speed around the base of the scrum and an instinct for a gap, and he was a creative player for others in the side. His selection as captain of the 1924 and 1928 tours bears testimony to his widely acknowledged powers of leadership and his tactical genius. But, like many scrum halves, he liked nothing better than to score. On his three tours Down Under he recorded 9 tries in 11 Test appearances against Australia and New Zealand, and in 1924 became one of only four British players to score a try in each Test of an Ashes series – the others were Johnny Thomas (1908–9), George Tyson (1908–9) and Ike Southward (1958).

Jonty Parkin.

As a captain, however, Jonty Parkin reigned supreme. There is no better testimony to his powers of leadership on and off the field than his guidance of his team to series victories over both Australia and New Zealand on his third tour for Great Britain, even though he played in only a few games due to injury. Alf Ellaby, a winger on that tour, bears witness to what Jonty Parkin achieved. 'Looking back at the names on the 1928 tour, it is now referred to as one of the great sides', he explained. 'But when the team was chosen the press gave us no chance and thought that there were only six players of Test class in the party. Poor diet and training on board ship left us in poor shape for the start of the tour and we won only two of the first six games.' Much of the credit for the transformation of these 'no-hopers' must go to Jonathan Parkin.

WAYNE PEARCE

b. 29.3.1960
Balmain, Australia

Before and during the Kangaroos' 1982 tour of Europe I had heard much of the power and strength of the new Australian second row sensation, Wayne Pearce. I was told of his enormous appetite for hard training, and how he ran up and down the full length of the flights of stairs in the Dragonara Hotel, Leeds, after strenuous training sessions under Kangaroo coach Frank Stanton; I had heard much of his speed.

Second row battering ram Wayne Pearce looks to offload the ball after a powerful run down the middle.

Lee Crooks
Colorsport

James Leuluai
Varley Picture Agency

ABOVE: Dean Bell
*Varley Picture
Agency*

OPPOSITE: Mal Meninga
*Associated Sports
Photography*

LEFT: (*left to right*) Brian
McTigue, Eric
Ashton and Billy
Boston
*Varley Picture
Agency*

Joe Lydon
Bob Thomas

After an hour's play in the opening Test match at Boothferry Park, Hull, he announced to 26,771 spectators at the ground and to millions of television viewers throughout the British Isles that he had indeed arrived. His power, his speed and his unbelievable standards of fitness were there for all to admire when he burst onto a Craig Young pass in his own half and shattered a wall of tacklers in front of him. His assault on the British line of defence can be likened to some form of battering ram breaking down one of our medieval castle walls which has been undisturbed for years. Not only did he score and take the Man of the Match award but his impact, and that of his team-mates, broke down our old-fashioned thinking on the game. Wayne Pearce, more than any other player, forced us to revalue our ideas on fitness and tactics and re-shaped thinking in the British game for many years after.

Out of the eight tries scored by Australia on that fateful day for British Rugby League four were scored by the forwards, one each for Les Boyd, Rod Reddy, Ray Price and Wayne Pearce. All of those pack stars, as well as the other two elder statesmen, Craig Young and Max Krilich, exhibited an athleticism and standard of fitness not seen in our game for 15 years. Their performances highlighted how lax we had allowed ourselves to become and threw into public ridicule the pathetic nature of British attempts at tackling. By the next Ashes series in 1984 in Australia, Wayne Pearce was still performing his feats of strength but at least we had duly noted the way forward and were making rapid attempts to rectify our problems.

Wayne Pearce, or 'Junior' as he is nicknamed by League fans, is the model professional. He portrays the ideal image for a modern, vibrant, healthy sport. His work as a development officer with youngsters has set many on the path not only to rugby glory but to maintaining the right standards off the field. Despite his prowess on the field, Wayne has remained loyal to Balmain, whom he joined in 1979. It is unusual for Australian League players, who are governed by two- and three-year contracts, to remain with one club. Many have cashed in on their talents with off-season spells in the British League, some of lesser ability assisting the French Rugby League teams. But Pearce has never strayed, nor has he considered Rugby League action in the British Isles as he is more than content to remain with Balmain for the foreseeable future.

ALAN PRESCOTT

b. 17.6.1927
Halifax, St Helens, Great
Britain

Alan Prescott, who in 1956 was the first ever forward to captain Great Britain and went on to be the tour captain of the Ashes-winning side in 1958, will always be remembered for one match, the second Test match at Brisbane in that 1958 tour. Skipper Alan Prescott knew that his side had to win the second Test, having lost the first Test 8–25. Such was his determination that, despite breaking his right arm, he volunteered to carry on because his team was down to 12 men at half time (David Bolton had left the field in the 17th minute with a broken collar bone and there were three other players also carrying injuries. To maintain morale he declared: 'I'll play on, tell nobody. I can be of nuisance value, the Australians will have to run round me'. His courage was unquestionable; the pain, when scrummaging in his prop position, can only be imagined, but somehow he led his side to a 25–18 victory. And following further success in the third Test, he was chaired in triumph around the Sydney Cricket Ground.

Alan was a prop forward whose 16-stone frame and thick shock of red hair was always in the thick of the action. He commanded the respect of all players and naturally emerged as a leader for both St Helens and Great Britain. Having begun his career with the St Marie's amateur club in Widnes, his home town, he joined Halifax in 1945 as a wing until, as his weight increased, he moved to the loose forward position. It was only when he was transferred to St Helens for the sum of £2,275 that his career as a prop forward really developed. He was persuaded against his will, by the St Helens coach Jim Sullivan, to play in the front row only when the team was shorthanded. He proved, much to his surprise, the ideal prop forward.

Although only 5 feet 10 inches tall Alan had exceptional pace, obviously a legacy of his days as a winger, and safe, skilful hands. His favourite ploy was to take the ball out wide, hurl his bulk at the opposition, force the gap and race upfield for 50 or 60 yards, often challenging the wingers to catch him. He was a noted tryscorer in an era when few forwards scored many, his best being the try he scored in St Helens' Challenge Cup final win over Halifax in 1956. That he won the Lance Todd Trophy was a fitting reward not only for his individual efforts but for his powers of leadership.

OPPOSITE: *Inspirational*
St Helens captain Alan
Prescott (left) leads his side
onto the field alongside Eric
Fraser of Warrington. Note
the resin on the front of his
jersey, used by Alan to
improve his grip on the ball.

At the end of his playing career Alan turned to coaching with St Helens and I have always been indebted to him as he was my first coach on signing professional terms from Rugby Union. He was a kindly and sympathetic man (perhaps too much so to gain the honours as a coach) who did much to pass on to me the benefit of his vast experience and to help me in my introduction to Rugby League.

Indeed that introduction was a hard one! I well remember leaving the pitch to inform Alan that I had dislocated my shoulder in a tackle

He looked under my jersey, lifted the shoulder pads and felt along the bone. I winced as he applied pressure. 'It's not too bad, Ray. Pack on the other side of the scrum.' Could anyone object to a man who had led his country to a Test triumph with a broken arm? No, he commanded everyone's respect.

RAY PRICE

b. 3.5.1953
Parramatta, Australia

As one who played international Rugby Union before transferring my allegiance to the League code, I can appreciate the difficulties of anyone starting out in a new code of rugby. The games are so different that for forwards the only similarity is the oval-shaped ball. In Union the forwards are expected to be the work horses about the field, ever chasing the ball or attempting to win it from rucks, mauls, line outs or scrums. Their chances of running with the ball, making individual tackles or passing the ball are very limited, save for the occasional foray from a back row forward. In League the forward is expected to be a far fitter specimen and more of an all-round player. He must be able to run, tackle and pass a ball, often at international level with the dexterity of a back. Many forwards originating in the Union code become adept at the League skills, a few flounder however when the emphasis is placed on individual skills rather than the unit skills of the Union code. Such changeovers of code are possibly best made by back row forwards or flankers in the Union game who have speed and handling abilities. Players like the Great Britain internationals of my own playing days, John Mantle and Charlie Renilson, admirably fitted the requirements. And in Australia there was none better than 'Mr Perpetual Motion', Parramatta's Ray Price.

Ray Price proved his worth as a Wallaby Union international in gaining seven caps between 1974 and 1976. His all-action play and dynamic tackling made him an ideal convert to the League code and his signing for Parramatta in 1976 was the start of a magnificent League career. Within three seasons of his conversion from Union to League he was so comfortably installed in his new code that he was awarded the Harry Sunderland Medal for the best player in the Ashes series of 1979, while his debut came in the previous year on the Kangaroo tour of Great Britain. What an amazing start to a League career! Ray Price was admirably suited to the tough Australian forward style and, like the brave First World War commanders, was at his best when he led from the front taking his troops, usually clad in green and gold, 'over the top'.

Typical of his 'never say die' attitude and his inspirational qualities was his play in the second Test at Wigan on the 1982 tour when Great Britain had a numerical advantage over the Kangaroos. Les Boyd, the Australian prop forward, had been dismissed from the field in the 35th minute for an offence on John Dalgreen, the Great Britain hooker. Ray Price, although suffering from a broken thumb which was to cost him his place in the third Test, led his 11 remaining colleagues into every tackle. He distributed the ball at every opportunity wherever he was on the field. He was swathed in plaster and bandages yet he hurled his 6 feet and 14-stone frame at anything that ran in a Great Britain jersey

until he had helped his side secure the Ashes trophy with a 27–6 victory. He led the forwards by example and rarely asked them to perform anything that he could not or would not do himself.

At club level, Parramatta were rewarded with performances of equal merit. In his record 258 First Grade appearances for the club, his displays were such that he was awarded the Rothmans Medal for the best and fairest player in the Sydney Premiership in 1979 and the Dally Messenger Award for the Player of the Year on two occasions, in 1979 and 1982. His fiery combative play on the field is echoed nowadays by Ray's tone in his weekly articles for the prestigious magazine *Rugby League Week* and in his regular radio commentaries throughout Sydney.

'Mr Perpetual Motion' Ray Price, at ease for once, on the receiving end of a lecture from referee Fred Lindop during Australia's 1982 tour of Great Britain.

WALLY PRIGG

b. 17.10.1908
Newcastle (Australia),
Australia

Alf Ellaby, Great Britain's elusive winger of the 1920s and 1930s, firmly believes that Wally Prigg was one of Australia's finest ball-playing loose forwards (or lock as our friends Down Under name the No. 13 position) and that, during his captaincy on the 1937 tour of Great Britain, he was the instigator of a style of Kangaroo forward play cultivated 30 years later by the likes of Ray Price and Johnny Raper. He insists that they were the first Australian Test team to introduce close support play among their forwards and to plan their midfield moves around such tactics. The *Sports Post* (Leeds) commented on their innovative style in discussing the Australian forward play after the first Test of 1937 at Headingley, Leeds: 'They gave us a perfect demonstration of the close passing and quick backing-up game. The men were always there in support. The straight short runs were driven in, and it really was

Wally Prigg perfected the art of close forward support play with his colleagues in the pack when he captained the 1937 Kangaroo tour.

remarkable how, even when men were more than half held, they managed to get the ball away to colleagues coming up at speed'.

Although only 5 feet 11 inches and 13 stones, not big for an Australian forward, Prigg was a very fast player who liked to break quickly from the scrum and indulge in passing bouts with his pack and half backs. He had the gift, so rare in a forward, of knowing exactly when to part with the ball to a colleague in support. He was not shy when near the opposition try line and he became a regular tryscorer both in club and international matches. His defensive work was also of a high calibre – he was an expert at moving up very quickly on the opposition stand off and stopping the flow of play before an attack could be mounted. Australia's most recent lock forwards, such as Ron Coote, Wayne Pearce and Bob Lindner, have tended to excel at running with the ball from wide positions and have concentrated on a strong cover defence. However, I imagine Wally Prigg, both in stature and style, to have been nearer to the all-action ball-handling players like Johnny Raper and Ray Price.

Ian Walsh is the only Australian forward to equal his achievement in playing in 12 Anglo/Australian Test matches between 1929 and 1937. Wally's captaincy during the 1937 Test series in England, although unsuccessful in terms of winning the Ashes, highlighted his powers of leadership and the respect in which he was held both by his contemporaries and, for many years to come, by those supporters who had the privilege of seeing him lead the Kangaroos.

NORMAN PROVAN

b. 18.12.1931
St George, Australia

When Tom Mitchell, the manager of the Great Britain tour of Australia and New Zealand in 1958, fought long and hard over the selection of his squad he had one task in mind: he needed a player of Vince Karalius's ability to help tame the tough Australian pack. In particular, he knew he must have the right forwards to subdue the dynamic second row pairing of Norman Provan and Kel O'Shea. It is well documented that Mr Mitchell managed eventually to include Vince in his tour party and that Great Britain eventually won the Ashes, but the reputation of Norman Provan, despite his team's defeat, was enhanced by all the attention he was paid by the opposition.

Inside his huge 6 feet 3-inch and $15\frac{1}{2}$-stone frame lay a durability and consistency which few forwards attain. Rugby League is a hard, often cruel, game in which players have to learn to absorb the knocks and cushion their bodies against wear and tear. So, to play at the highest club and Test levels for 14 seasons as Norman Provan did with St George and Australia from 1951 to 1965, is testimony not only to a player's ability but also to his endurance and strength. In partnership with his usual international second row mate, Kel O'Shea, Norman was a difficult stumbling block for any Great Britain pack seeking to gain midfield dominance. He could pass a ball well, or burst through a gap on attack and he would tackle the hardest and meanest of opponents. He enjoyed considerable success in the two World Cup competitions of 1954 and 1957 but sadly for British spectators, on his only Kangaroo tour of England a series of injuries caused him to miss all three Test matches.

Whatever Norman's deeds on the field when wearing a green and gold jersey, his exploits when playing for St George in the Sydney Premiership will always be recalled by historians of the game. As he represented them in 263 First Grade matches, the name of Provan became synonymous with the famous 'Dragons' club for the most successful 14 seasons in the history of any Australian club, during which time they became virtually unbeatable. He played a considerable part in the club's amazing run of winning 11 Sydney Grand Finals between 1956 and 1966, playing in a record ten finals himself and missing only the 11th. In 1962 he took over as player-coach at St George and coached the side to four of those historic wins. Perhaps the most momentous of them was the 1965 final against Western Suburbs. Although there had been torrential rain for two days prior to the match a crowd of nearly 70,000 still flocked to the Sydney Cricket Ground to watch Norman Provan lead his side to a narrow 8–3 victory over Wests, who fielded two of the strongest forwards in the game in Kel O'Shea and Noel Kelly. Although they had lost twice to Wests in earlier rounds of the competition, Norman's expertise on the big occasion triumphed.

As a forward myself, and knowing what the game demands both physically and mentally, I can well appreciate the qualities of Norman Provan. Some players arrive on the rugby stage with the brilliance of a meteorite but leave and burn out just as quickly. Others, like the stars, seem to shine for ever and are looked up to as models of consistency. Such a player was Norman Provan: he set his standards and kept to them. Although he never had the good fortune to captain Australia he was one of the most inspirational captains of St George, taking the club to peaks never before or since attained by any club anywhere in the world.

I vividly remember from my schooldays in the 1950s the powerful breaks of Norman Provan, one of the greatest forwards ever produced by the famous Sydney St George club.

JOHNNY RAPER

b. 12.4.1939
Newtown, St George,
Australia

I watched this great Australian loose forward for the first time at clos
quarters on the Kangaroo tour of Britain in 1963 when I was seated o
the Great Britain reserves bench for the second Test at Swinton. As n
substitutes were allowed in those days, I was given ample opportunit
to squirm at the 50–12 thrashing that Australia handed out to Grea
Britain as well as to appreciate at the same time the running skills o
John Raper. He had a hand in every try as he seemed to pop u
everywhere on the pitch whenever there was a threat of a breakdown o

movement. His tackling, his passing, his tactical awareness were all at the level I would expect of one of the greatest loose forwards and yet it was his running which impressed me most.

Five years later, when he was captain of Australia in the World Cup tournament, our paths crossed again, this time on the pitch itself in a very encounter between Great Britain and Australia at the Sydney Cricket Ground. I remember being made to look helpless (and possibly hopeless!) when he mesmerised me with a shimmy of his body and raced past to set up a try. He used to carry the ball in both hands, held high up away from his chest, the perfect position from which to pass out of any oncoming tackles. Furthermore he would move the ball from side to side and developed a darting, weaving run which was most disconcerting to any defenders. If you stood still on your heels waiting for him you would miss him as he veered around you. Only if you moved towards him, like a soccer goalkeeper moving forward to cut down the goalscorer's range of shot, would you have the satisfaction of stopping him. He stood me on my heels that day and, in a Rugby League player's jargon, 'beat me all ends up'.

John was a very determined competitor and was able to win through when the odds were stacked against him. At regular intervals in his nine-year Test career from 1959 to 1968 he suffered great pain from back trouble and would have to take to the field with a type of corset strapped round him as protection. Alan Clarkson, for 33 years a highly respected journalist with the *Sydney Morning Herald*, possibly best described Johnny Raper when he declared that: 'If a horse had a heart like his he'd be capable of winning both legs of the daily double'.

This former policeman, with Wally Prigg, was the only forward to make three Australian tours to Europe. He spent his first two seasons in League with the now defunct Newtown club from 1957. However, his best rugby performances came when he joined St George in 1959, where he gained many successes in Sydney Grand Finals.

John's international career included two Test caps against the South African Rugby League side, which makes him a rarity among players. When South Africa briefly flirted with Rugby League in the early 1960s they toured Australia with a side led by former Union player Dawie Ackermann, which included converts to the British Rugby League scene such as Fred Griffiths (Wigan) and Alan Skene (Wakefield Trinity). Sadly, their lack of success failed to ignite the interest of the public back in South Africa. However, the tour did provide yet another chapter in the illustrious international career of Johnny Raper.

OPPOSITE: *Johnny Raper, an instinctive footballer and a devastating tackler, was without doubt the finest loose forward I ever played against.*

MAL REILLY

b. 19.1.1948
Castleford, Manly, Great
Britain

In September 1968 I travelled over to Hull Kingston Rovers as th
confident captain of the Lancashire team to play Yorkshire in the Ros
match. Having had a successful World Cup tour with Great Britain i
Australia earlier in the summer I had eased myself only gently back int
training for the coming season. I was not expecting to have to exer
myself too much in a match so early in the season. Some hope, for
and my team were hit by a whirlwind in the shape of a young man
had never come across on a League pitch before: Castleford and York
shire loose forward Mal Reilly. Although we lost only 10–5, this youn

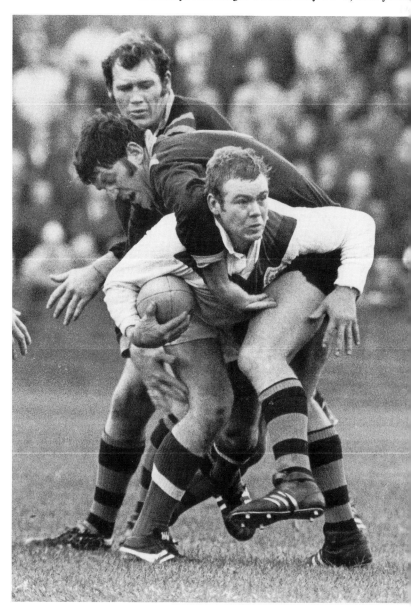

Malcolm Reilly's
determination and strength to
break a tackle can be seen in
his all-action display in the
1970 Ashes series.

player ripped holes in our midfield defence and knocked us unceremoniously to the floor with the bone-shattering tackles which were to be his trademark for years to come. Mal Reilly, who had been signed by Castleford in 1967 from the amateurs at Kippax Welfore, arrived on the Rugby League scene that day. Wherever he played over the next 15 seasons he wrought havoc among the opposition.

Within 12 months of my first encounter with him he had won the Lance Todd Trophy in Castleford's Challenge Cup final defeat of Salford. By the conclusion of the 1969–70 season he had helped to defeat Wigan in a second Challenge Cup final appearance and was on his way to destroy the Australians' Ashes chances in the Test series Down Under that summer. Such were his performances on Great Britain's Ashes-winning tour that it was not long before Mal was in demand with the rich Sydney clubs and, like Phil Lowe, Roger Millward, Tommy Bishop and others, he joined the list of British players tempted to play in Australia.

Castleford temporarily lost his services for four seasons when, for an overseas fee of £15,000, a record at the time, he joined the famous Manly club in Sydney. And to what effect for Manly! The hard, dry grounds of Sydney suited a loose forward of the pace of Malcolm Reilly and the strong emphasis on defence in the Sydney League competition meant that he was able to call into play one of the strongest parts of his rugby repertoire. Australia also gave him the opportunity to display his ball-handling skills and to bring a touch of old-fashioned British loose forward play to the Sydney competition. Most Australian loose forwards of the modern era have tended to be strong-running, hard-tackling players not especially renowned for their creative play. Only John Raper, or me, had all the attributes of a complete loose forward in the British mould. Thus, with Mal Reilly up front in the pack, and with the skills of Bobby Fulton and Graham Eadie behind, it was no surprise that Manly won two consecutive Sydney Premiership finals, defeating Eastern Suburbs and Cronulla in 1972 and 1973 respectively.

Mal Reilly added another dimension to his rugby skills when, on his return as player-coach to Castleford in 1975, he began to use a high kick to good effect. In spite of the fact that he was suffering from a long-standing knee injury, Mal became the ball-playing creative force behind the strong Castleford pack and his use of Eddie Waring's 'up and under' kick brought many a try for his side. Wherever he played, or for whomever he played, Mal was a winner who wanted just one thing from his rugby – success. His nine Great Britain caps were scant reward for such a great loose forward, and he missed out on further awards during his stay at Manly. He won numerous trophies as Castleford's coach – further evidence of his shrewd rugby brain and tactical planning. He fully deserved the honour of becoming the Great Britain coach for the 1988 Lions tour – it was no less than a player and a coach of his ability warranted.

JOHNNY RING

b. 13.11.1900
Wigan, Rochdale Hornets,
Great Britain

*A record-breaker in both
codes, Johnny Ring played a
vital role in Wigan's success
of the 1920s, establishing
their current record number
of tries in a season of 62 in
1925–26.*

The oft-quoted saying that 'it takes a good centre to make a good wing' is very true in Rugby League, but occasionally a partnership comes together where such are both players' abilities that they dovetail into an unstoppable attacking machine. The partnership of Tommy Howley who hailed from Ebbw Vale, and Johnny Ring, who joined Wigan from Aberavon in 1922, was one in which both players had such a complete understanding of each other's play that they were devastating to any club opposing Wigan in the 1920s. Tommy Howley was a most skilful centre who quickly appreciated the outstanding skills of his wing, Johnny Ring. He was the architect of many of Ring's vast number of tries by giving him the early ball. Ring's talents did the rest.

Johnny Ring had gained a Welsh Rugby Union cap and set the current individual Welsh tryscoring record of 76 in a season with Aberavon in 1919–20 before he journeyed north to entertain the fans at Wigan. He had also represented Swansea City for two seasons as their centre forward. However, it was the cash offer to join Wigan that tempted him to leave Wales, since it allowed him to engage an eminent surgeon to attend to his lame sister. Whatever his reasons for signing, the name of Johnny Ring was never out of the Rugby League record books as try followed try. He became Wigan's record tryscorer, setting a figure of 62 tries in season 1925–26 and also scored seven tries on three occasions, in matches against the two amateur sides Flimby and Fothergill and Pemberton Rovers and against Salford. Such feats also gave him the tryscoring record for an individual match, with Billy Boston and Green Vigo, who also achieved the total of seven tries in a match. During four seasons between 1922 and 1926 he was to top the Rugby League tryscoring charts on four consecutive occasions with figures of 41, 49, 54 and 63 tries – a wonderful record of consistency.

It is surprising that he was awarded only two Great Britain caps when he reigned supreme for ten seasons as the leading tryscorer in the game. He did tour Australasia with Great Britain in 1924, emerging with the most tries, 23 from only 15 appearances on the trip, but he played in only one of the six Test matches against Australia and New Zealand. Although his talents were not always appreciated by Great Britain's selectors, his pace down the wing, his body sway and his delicate sidestep were more than appreciated by those who had to face him on a field. His uncanny ability to thread his way past defenders was observed by a future Great Britain captain, Gus Risman, when he went to watch him immediately after he had signed Rugby League terms from the Cardiff Rugby Union Club. He commented: 'In the first game of Rugby League I ever saw, Wigan v Broughton Rangers, I observed Johnny Ring ballet dancing and tightrope walking his way down the touchline from his own 25 to place the ball between the posts'.

GUS RISMAN

b. 21.3.1911
Salford, Workington Town,
Great Britain

Gus Risman, who attended the same school as Billy Boston in Tiger Bay, Cardiff, was a softly spoken full back or centre who was destined for greatness from the day he 'played with old magazines tied up with bits of string in the streets of Cardiff'. It was no surprise to rugby followers in Wales when he was signed by Salford on 31st January 1929, just two months prior to his 18th birthday, for the sum of £152, payable over the year. What value he gave to Salford and Rugby League! His 17 seasons at Salford coincided with the arrival of the legendary New Zealand manager Lance Todd, who made the 'Red Devils', as they are known, the premier club in the land under the astute captaincy of Gus Risman. Whether at full back, his favourite position, or at centre, Gus was the supreme tactician, displaying a farseeing vision of the game which allowed him to direct operations on the field for even the most gifted of players alongside him. Every possible trophy found its way, at some period, into the Salford show cabinet while Gus's individual skills brought him every honour in the game.

As a centre his first priority was to serve his winger with precision-timed passes, while as a full back he was always alert for the attacking options. His career spanned 27 seasons, during which time he managed to score over 3,000 points. However, despite this, at both Salford (1929–46) and Workington (1946–54) he was more famed for creating tries for others than for his own tryscoring and goalkicking prowess. Naturally such talent was rewarded with Great Britain tours Down Under in 1932 and 1936 and his powers of leadership were acknowledged when he was appointed captain of the 1946 Great Britain touring party.

This tour was hastily conceived so as to renew Rugby League relations between the two continents as quickly as possible when war ceased, so the party travelled in the only available boat, an aircraft carrier named *The Indomitable*. Despite being 'dumped off the boat at Fremantle, Western Australia' and being forced to 'travel for a week across the Nullaboor Plain to Sydney', Gus overcame such adversities to lead his touring party to an Ashes success.

Many who have had the rare distinction of playing a Test match against Australia at the age of 35 years, as Gus did on that 1946 trip, would no doubt feel highly pleased with themselves and settle for a quiet retirement. Not Gus Risman. He still had the energy to lead a new club, Workington Town, into the Rugby League as player-manager and, having guided them to a Championship win over Warrington in 1951, was still fit enough to lead them onto the field at Wembley at the age of 41 years, a record for any player in a Challenge Cup final. His fitness in this toughest of sports was truly staggering, allowing him to compete in five Anglo/Australian Test series between 1932 and 1946.

Notwithstanding all his achievements in Rugby League, Gus was

At both club and international level Gus Risman was a visionary captain, leading every team under his command to success.

especially proud to be selected to captain Wales at both codes of rugby when, as well as guesting with Dewsbury, Leeds and Bradford League clubs during the Second World War, he led Wales in five wartime Union internationals. What fine rugby must have been played during those war years when the Rugby Union's anti-professional stance was relaxed and players such as Trevor Foster, Ike Owens and Doug Phillips from League could play alongside Bleddyn Williams, Haydn Tanner and ex-R.F.U. secretary Robin Prescott. How sad that it takes a war to bring such rugby talent together!

ALBERT ROSENFELD

b. 28.7.1885
Eastern Suburbs,
Huddersfield, Wakefield
Trinity, Bradford Northern,
Australia

I have recorded elsewhere the debt owed by the League code to many ex-Union stars, but few have achieved as much as this little man. Albert Rosenfeld, born into a Jewish family in Sydney, struggled with his contemporaries to found the Rugby League code, both in Australia and later in Britain. I describe him as 'little' for, despite his incredible tryscoring feats as a winger for Huddersfield, he was only 5 feet 5 inches

Albert Rosenfeld's 1913–14 record of 80 tries in a season is unlikely ever to be surpassed. But for the intervention of the First World War, who knows what feats he might have accomplished?

and 11 stones 8 pounds when he toured Britain with the first side from Down Under. Barely the size of a scrum half, he must have possessed unusual skills to weave his way past the many would-be tacklers and he needed immense strength to shrug off the hordes of covering forwards. Indeed, his original position in that historic first Rugby League game in Australia against the paid New Zealanders on 17th August 1907 was at stand off.

Rugby League in Australia was founded that day and, with the creation of a league in Sydney, it was not long before Rosenfeld, now playing at half back for Eastern Suburbs, was on his way to England with the Kangaroos' first tour in 1908–09 season. Although, along with three other players, he was only a late addition to the 34-strong party, having been included after a public outcry, he was determined to be fit when he arrived at Dover. And what a novel fitness schedule his team manager, James Giltinan, employed! Along with his five playing colleagues from Eastern Suburbs he took it in turns to work a shift stoking the boilers on the ship *Macedonia* as it made its leisurely way across the high seas – a far cry from the quick air flight enjoyed by modern tourists.

Few people in Britain were prepared for the sensational impact the little man made when he signed for Huddersfield at the conclusion of that first overseas tour from Australia in which, despite 15 appearances, he scored only five tries. Once he had settled in at Fartown, Huddersfield, he became accustomed to scoring that number in a single match. Albert Rosenfeld celebrated his debut at Huddersfield on 11th September 1909 with two tries and was to join one of the greatest and most prolific points-scoring threequarter lines of all time when his name was added to the programme alongside those of Moorhouse, Gleeson and Wagstaff.

Albert's tryscoring feats are truly incredible and, but for the intervention of the First World War, who knows what he might have accomplished. With totals of 40, 78, 56, 80 and 56 tries scored in an amazing five seasons from 1910 to 1915 he became the only player to top the tryscoring charts for five consecutive seasons. Although he enjoyed brief spells with Wakefield Trinity and Bradford Northern before he retired in 1924, his reputation was earned at Fartown and will possibly remain forever in that staggering, world-record total of 80 tries from 42 matches in season 1913–14. Incidentally, all those tries were scored in the Huddersfield colours, there being no representative honours available to him.

Although two of Albert Rosenfeld's countrymen have come nearest to breaking his record number of tries – Lionel Cooper (Huddersfield) with 71 and Brian Bevan (Warrington) with 72 – I doubt whether the total will now ever be beaten. In the modern style of play, where the wing does not receive the amount of running chances he once did, the task should prove impossible. I have no doubt, then, that 'Rozzy's' name will grace the record books forever.

MARTIN RYAN

b. 26.8.1923
Wigan, Great Britain

Martin Ryan, supported by a Wigan colleague, wrongfoots the defence in a country game during Great Britain's tour of Australia in 1950.

When that masterly duo at half back, Tommy Bradshaw and Cec Mountford, were running through their repertoire of tricks in midfield for Wigan in the immediate post-War years, there was an opening for an adventurous full back to make the most of their exciting play. That full back was Martin Ryan, a local ex-amateur signing from the Wigan St Joseph's club, who so stamped himself on full back play that his style proved to be the norm for the next four decades. If Mountford made one of his piercing, darting breaks, there was a need for a running full back to continue the movement and create the overlap for his wing. Alternatively, if Mountford elected to send the ball at pace along the threequarter line, there was an opportunity for a full back to link up on the outside between the centre and his wing. Martin Ryan had the pace, flair and strength to fulfil the role and thus established a running style of full back so different from that of the previous custodians of the No. 1 jersey, except perhaps Jim Brough of Leeds and Great Britain.

Signed by Wigan on 12th October 1940 as a centre, Martin cited his versatility in those early post-War years as being the major factor that helped him to break out of the previous mould of full back play: 'I signed as a centre, played at scrum half and loose forward', he explained. 'So it was my natural inclination to run with the ball whenever I had the opportunity, even though I was frequently catching it at the back'.

Such was his positional play and ability to sell a 'dummy' to the tightest of defences that it was natural that he should be selected to represent his country on two tours Down Under in 1946 and 1950. Sadly, a groin injury restricted him to four appearances on his first trip. Nevertheless, whether at home or abroad his facility for starting movements from deep in his own half served his country well at Test level. A scribe writing of his display in the second Test v Australia at Swinton in 1948 when he helped Great Britain to a 16–7 win perhaps best sums up how he was the vital cog in a well-oiled team: 'Ryan gave his best Test match display. He was the perfect engine for the perfect machine. He started movements in clockwork fashion'. And yet, despite all Martin Ryan's renown for his attacking abilities, he did not neglect the basic role of the full back as the last line of defence. Jack Winstanley, in his book *The History of Wigan R.L.F.C.*, pictured him 'shepherding opposing wingmen into a position where they became as harmless as sheep in a pen'. He was further blessed with a vision that few players are able to attain.

Since his retirement in 1952 Martin has rarely allowed his affection for Rugby League to lapse, serving at various stages with distinction on the Wigan Board of Directors and influencing his company to provide the sport with much-appreciated sponsorship.

GARRY SCHOFIELD

b. 1.7.1965
Hull, Balmain, Leeds, Great
Britain

Garry Schofield, or 'The Poacher' as he is known on account of his uncanny ability to score tries from seemingly impossible positions, was destined to join any list of great players from the day he made his debut for Hull in August 1983. His pedigree had been illustrated when, as captain of the Great Britain amateur youth tour to New Zealand that summer, the Hunslet Parkside junior impressed everyone Down Under. Within 12 months he was again the toast of Australia, only this time as the youngest ever professional player to accompany Great Britain on tour at the tender age of 18 years 10 months. On Humberside he had thrilled the Hull fans by becoming the youngest player ever to top the game's tryscoring chart with 38 in an incredible first season. All that and he was not yet 19! More records followed when, in the process of passing his career century of tries while still only 21, he equalled the British individual tryscoring record against New Zealand with four tries in the second Test of 1985. His tryscoring deeds have been truly staggering and with many more seasons of play to come, further records will surely tumble to this modest player.

Such talent as Garry Schofield possesses is a rare commodity and, when that talent becomes available, it inevitably commands a high price. In fact, another world record! When Hull ran into financial difficulties at the beginning of the 1987–88 season they were forced to sell their most important assets, Lee Crooks and Garry Schofield, to Leeds. Garry commanded a world record fee of £178,250, but soon showed the large Headingley crowd that he had not finished his tryscoring feats. He registered two tries on the scoreboard in his debut for Leeds against Auckland on 25th October 1987.

Many critics, ever looking to dampen any undue praise accorded to a star player, acknowledge Schofield's uncanny ability to score tries from the most difficult of positions at the most crucial of times, yet they often hint that he is not a creative centre. That will come. There is no doubt that he creates tries with his keen positional sense and electrifying bursts off the mark. Two spells of play with Balmain in the defensively-minded Sydney League in Australia also illustrated how well this ideally-built 6 feet and 13-stone centre can tackle. But their approach did not prevent him from scoring tries too.

Some players can hit top form at club level but consistently fail to produce the same form in the international game. But with Garry Schofield the more important the event the better he seems to play. His tryscoring average at international level of almost one per appearance puts him on target for Mick Sullivan's record 40 tries between 1954 and 1963 but, whatever his eventual total at his retirement, few tries will give more encouragement than his five in the 1986 Anglo/Australian Test series which helped to relieve the gloom of yet another British

'The Poacher' in action. Great Britain centre Garry Schofield lives up to his nickname as he thunders joyfully towards a try against France in 1988.

series whitewash. This former bricklayer is now a full-time professional player with an even more glorious future ahead of him. His former Leeds and Great Britain coach, Maurice Bamford declared: 'By the time he is in his mid-20s I believe he will have become one of the all-time greats'. Many of us would say that Garry Schofield has already joined that illustrious list.

CHARLIE SEELING

b. 14.5.1883
Wigan

Wigan have always been the most cosmopolitan of the British clubs, attracting players from far and wide. They have found few more loyal servants than the many Kiwis, such as Len Mason, Brian Nordgren, Cec Mountford and Kevin Iro, who have come from New Zealand to find fame at Central Park. All have followed a path first trodden by Lance Todd, the celebrated player and manager who gave his name to the Man of the Match award at the Challenge Cup final, and Charlie Seeling, the famous ex-All Black forward. Lance Todd, who had toured Britain with the first New Zealand Rugby League team in 1907–08, and Charlie Seeling, capped 11 times for the All Blacks Union team and a member of their tour to Great Britain in 1905–06, were the first to establish the association of New Zealanders with Wigan. Both men were instrumental in making Wigan the premier club in the land prior to the First World War.

Charlie Seeling, who enjoyed 13 successful seasons with Wigan, was one of the few All Black Union men to play Rugby League in Britain.

Charlie Seeling, despite never having represented his country at League, remains to this day one of the best forwards ever produced by New Zealand. Born in Auckland, Charlie soon developed into a tough tackling, all-action Union forward who attracted the League scouts in increasing numbers. Having played in the centre before moving to the prop position in Rugby Union, he possessed a rare turn of speed and a steady pair of hands with which to handle a ball. These attributes soon attracted Wigan representatives who, delighted with their capture of Lance Todd two years earlier, promptly signed him in January 1910. Nor were they disappointed, for Charlie indicated the rich harvest that the club would reap with a tryscoring debut in the club's 67–0 annihilation of Merthyr (now extinct) on 5th February 1910. Lance Todd, by now very much at home in Lancashire, also helped himself to a try.

Mostly figuring in the loose forward position and, later in his career, in the second row, Charlie Seeling spent over 13 seasons with Wigan and developed such an affection for the town that he was to remain in charge of a local hostelry until his death in 1966. In over 200 first team matches Charlie developed into a rarity among pre-First World War forwards – a tryscorer. In those early days of Rugby League the forwards tended to be the ball-getters at well over 60 or 70 scrums a match and then, when in possession, they were expected to release it to the backs as quickly as possible. Not Charlie Seeling! In the four seasons between 1910 and 1914, when the outbreak of war seriously interrupted the development of his career, he scored 54 tries. Even in the modern game, in which forwards are given far greater freedom to roam the pitch and are expected to be much faster than their counterparts in the past, such a total is not achieved by many internationals.

The failure of the New Zealand authorities to include overseas players in their teams and the scarcity of international competition in those early days prevented Charlie Seeling from becoming a double international at both Union and League. But he is still considered by many to be one of New Zealand's greatest exports.

BILLY SMITH

b. 12.7.1942
St George, Australia

Take a close look at any successful club or international side and you will find a successful partnership at work between the loose forward and the scrum half. These two positions, particularly in the modern game, are the engine room of any great side. The players who occupy these positions are usually at the heart of all attacks, handle the ball more times than anyone else on the pitch and play a big part in a team's defensive plans. Partnerships like Alex Murphy and Vince Karalius for St Helens and Great Britain or Ray Price and Peter Sterling for Parramatta and Australia readily spring to mind as being among the best in the history of the game. I would suggest that the St George and Australian pairing of Johnny Raper and Billy Smith is also worthy of consideration as one of the greatest of pairings.

A loose forward must have a complete understanding with his scrum half at the base of the scrum so that the timing of their moves is perfect. Both must know when to pick up the ball at the base of the scrum and launch the other on an attack, often down the blind side of a scrum. Each player must know instinctively how and when to follow the other in open play so as to seize onto the short pass, usually slipped out of the tackle, to the partner who is in the clear. In short, there must be a telepathic understanding between them.

Billy Smith, as one half of the dynamic Raper/Smith partnership, was an outstanding player making good use of his short, stocky stature and 11-stone 7-pound frame. At his peak in the 1960s he was an extremely rugged character, rather in the Keith Holman mould, most suited to the close in-fighting around the base of the scrum. His clashes around the scrums in the 1966 Test series, for which he won the Man of the Series Award, with Great Britain's tempestuous little scrum half, Tommy Bishop, produced some lively exchanges. And they continued the battle in the World Cup competition of 1968.

Billy was a constructive player and a great thinker on the game, always in partnership with Johnny Raper at the centre of both St George's and Australia's tactical plans. His footballing ability was further illustrated by the fact that he was able to play not only at scrum half but even, on occasion, at stand off for his St George club for whom he made over 300 First Grade appearances.

His commitment was brought home to me when I lined up for 'Great Britain Past' against 'Australia Past' at the North Sydney Oval in 1988. This exhibition game, designed to please fans with the sight of players of yesteryear, suddenly took on a competitive edge when Billy had the ball. He ran with the fervour of his youth and whenever Great Britain were in possession he harassed continually. Such was his enthusiasm that he had to retire early having broken his ribs, even though it was only a game of touch rugby.

Billy Smith was a tough little nugget of a player whose distribution of the ball from the scrum half position launched innumerable attacks for Australia and St George.

KURT SORENSON

b. 8.11.1956
Mt Wellington, Wigan,
Cronulla, Eastern Suburbs,
Widnes, New Zealand

Rugby League was to gain when Kurt Sorenson's Danish seafaring forefathers jumped ship in Tonga and finally settled in Auckland, New Zealand. Surely the spirit of the rough and ready sailors of yesteryear is still to be traced in the tough, uncompromising play of Kurt, one of the Kiwis' finest post-War forwards.

Kurt's 16-stone bulk is packed into a height of only 5 feet 9 inches, a physique which presents a fearsome sight on the field. Given his astonishing speed, it is no surprise that he is most difficult to stop, even for the most determined of tacklers. At both club and international level, Kurt Sorenson has regularly been the battering ram to break down the tightest of defences, whether bouncing opposition forwards off his considerable frame or surging through a gap down the flanks and leaving a centre floundering, unable to match the speed of this powerful second row or prop forward. Such tactics at Naughton Park, Widnes enabled him to lead the English club to the most prestigious honour in the game, the championship of Division One in 1987–88. His fierce, and at times intimidating, tackling warned off any would-be champions from over-exerting themselves against Widnes whenever they cared to travel to Naughton Park.

Having played Union as a schoolboy, Kurt's ability to dominate a game by his physical strength was amply illustrated when he represented the Mt Wellington side in Auckland as a 15-year-old, playing League alongside adults. His speed is also indicated by the fact that his first position was at centre. But it was not long before, as a forward, he had gained full Auckland selection at 17 years of age, and a New Zealand international cap in the 1975 World Cup tournament, in which he was pitted against the equally fearsome Jim Mills, the Welsh prop forward and now Kurt's committeeman at Widnes. A spell with Wigan in season 1976–77 under the coaching of the legendary Great Britain forward Vince Karalius completed his apprenticeship in the pack.

Never afraid to challenge the authorities whenever their rulings threatened to hinder the development of his career, Kurt Sorenson chose to have a year away from Rugby League in 1978 when a ban was imposed on players signing for overseas clubs on short-term contracts. After living in Australia for a year he was eligible to play for Cronulla in Sydney, gaining considerable success between 1979 and 1983, and later for Eastern Suburbs and Widnes. At all three clubs, such was Kurt's reputation that it was only natural that the Kiwi coach Graham Lowe should make him the centrepiece of his Test packs against Great Britain and Australia in the 1980s.

Although he is a modest and quiet man off the field, Kurt has invariably led from the front in many a fierce forward battle, never once taking a backward step. In his capacity as assistant player-coach at

Widnes he has encouraged young forwards like Paul Hulme, Phil McKenzie and Richard Eyres to develop their own styles of play. And, whenever youth may have been found wanting in the heat of the forward exchanges, he has set the example with his leadership and forceful attacking play. In all respects he has been a mighty forward and one of the cornerstones in the pre-eminence of New Zealand Rugby League in the 1980s.

Few prop forwards have had a greater influence on the British game than fiery Kiwi Kurt Sorenson. His leadership from the front made him a forward to be feared at Test level in the 1980s.

RAY STEHR

b. 24.1.1913
Eastern Suburbs, Australia

Clashes between Great Britain and Australia, whether at rugby or cricket, hockey or athletics, are invariably hard fought and are often accompanied by the most heated of exchanges. Such is the intense rivalry in sport between the two nations that occasionally those exchanges erupt beyond the rules of true sportsmanship. Rugby League Test matches at times walk a delicate tightrope between hard, uncompromising play and foul play, which can never be condoned. And yet those players who overstep that fragile borderline are looked upon with a mixture of adulation and amusement by their followers. Their rough tactics arouse the anger of the crowds but they stir the passions of their supporters. Such a player was the fiery Eastern Suburbs and Australian Test prop Ray Stehr, who achieved the dubious distinction of becoming the only man to be sent off twice in a Test series.

The tough and uncompromising Ray Stehr has passed into Australian folklore as one of the roughest forwards ever to wear the green and gold jersey.

190

Ray Stehr's clashes with Great Britain's Nat Silcock in the first Test of 1936 and with Jack Arkwright in the third Test of the same series resulted in him being dismissed from the field on both occasions. These dismissals gave him a certain notoriety and indeed, with his constant chattering at referees, he was a most difficult customer to control on a rugby field. Yet his behaviour, often at times a little wild, must not lessen his reputation as a strong prop forward equal to the best of his era. At 14 stones and 5 feet 11 inches he was not the biggest of prop forwards, but he was one of the fastest in his day and enjoyed running with the ball in his hands. It was a common sight to see him appear in the threequarter line, linking up in a passing movement with the centres.

Ray shook the Rugby League fraternity in Sydney when he made his First Grade debut for Eastern Suburbs against Newcastle in 1928 at the unbelievable age of 15 years. It is difficult to imagine a forward so young being able to make his debut in the hardest of team games among mature men. Yet his record-breaking entry into Rugby League certainly highlighted his physical prowess and his determination. And yet, but for a Chinese herbal doctor from Sydney, he would have been lying on his back paralysed from the age of eight. When a blood clot formed on his hip, he was encased in plaster for 12 months, unable to move, leaving the doctors in a quandary as to how to cure him. A Chinese herbalist with various potions came to the rescue and managed to dissolve the clot, and thus Ray Stehr was able to begin his career in rugby. His six Anglo/Australian Test appearances between 1933 and 1938 included two tours of Great Britain in 1933 and 1937 and one to New Zealand in 1935, due reward for his wholehearted play and a tribute to the skills of the healer from China.

Unfortunately Ray's style of play and especially his outspoken comments as a radio commentator regularly landed him in trouble with the Australian Board of Control. This has detracted somewhat from many critics' estimation of his talents. There is no doubt that he was uncompromising in his play and often harsh in his views, and yet beneath his rugged exterior he had respect for those as tough as himself. Every Christmas until his death in June 1983 he sent a card to the former Great Britain forward, Jack Arkwright, at his home in St Helens.

PETER STERLING

b. 16.9.1960
Parramatta, Hull,
Australia

In my lifetime I never thought that I would actually play with, play against or watch another scrum half the equal of the St Helens and Great Britain maestro, Alex Murphy. He possessed every single attribute you would feed into a computer if you wished to design a blueprint for the perfect scrum half. Yet when I watched Peter Sterling's performances, first on the 1982 Kangaroo tour and then his efforts on the 1986 tour and his superb displays during his 28 matches for Hull in 1984–85, I readily admit that I saw his near equal. I must be frank and use the word 'near', for Peter Sterling to my mind is slightly behind Alex Murphy in one respect: speed. Murphy was by far the faster off the mark and the quicker over any distance on a field, but in every other respect I would judge Peter Sterling to be his equal.

Peter's flowing blond hair immediately causes him to stand out in any match, but his work rate both around the scrums and in loose play quickly brings him to the centre of attention. He is an organiser of play, at his best when he is nearest to the point of distribution of the ball and a tactical genius on attack, whether launching attacks with passes or kicks. He is a magnificent motivator, unceasing in his urging on of his team-mates and always, when captain, leads from the front. Nor does his tiny frame – he is only 5 feet 8 inches tall and weighs barely 11 stones – cause him to shirk his share of the tackling. His tackle count in a match is always high and the vast majority of his tackles are perfectly executed around the legs. He is the busy bee of rugby, superbly fit, and able to turn his hand to any skill on a field.

Peter's performances for Hull in the Silk Cut Challenge Cup semi-final of 1985 and the subsequent replay against Castleford will always be firmly etched in my mind. They were bettered only by his gallant effort in defeat later in the Wembley final against Wigan. When all seemed lost and Wigan looked to be coasting away with the game, he alone prodded Hull back on course to come within inches of providing a sudden shock. He chivvied his pack in front of him, kept them moving forward with sensible kicks to touch and sent them on midfield runs with his judicious distribution. This little man with a big heart sat Hull on his shoulders and brought them back into the match by his sheer determination and willpower, only to see them fail at the last gasp by 28–24.

At the Fairfield Patrician Brothers School it was obvious that Peter was a future international player although it was a huge surprise when, still an 18-year-old schoolboy, he took his place at full back for Parramatta against Manly in a replayed Premiership semi-final match in 1978. That debut was to herald a long and triumphant connection with the 'Eels'. Peter contributed to their first Sydney Premiership title in 1981 with a 20–11 win over Newtown and went on to feature prominently

The creative role of Peter Sterling, the scrum half par excellence of the 1980s, behind the mighty Australian Test packs was responsible for the nation's total domination of world rugby during this period.

in many other Grand Finals throughout the 1980s, helping himself to the Rothmans Medal in 1986 and 1987 as the best and fairest player in the competition.

His total dedication to the game of Rugby League, his unique rugby skills and above all his exemplary sportsmanship on the field of play have earned him the respect of players and spectators alike throughout the world. He has surely cast doubts on the oft-quoted rugby truism that 'a good big 'un will always beat a good little 'un'. Peter Sterling is such a unique 'little 'un' that he can beat any of the 'big 'uns' without too much effort.

JIM SULLIVAN

b. 2.12.1903
Wigan, Great Britain

Jim Sullivan, in one of his favourite roles – as coach and trainer – attends to Jack Hilton's leg before a match. Hilton is now a director of Wigan.

When Wigan signed Jim Sullivan, a 17-year-old youth from the Cardiff Rugby Union Club for a record-equalling fee of £750, there were many in that rugby-mad town who doubted the wisdom of such a gamble. Twenty five years later with 25 Test caps, an incredible tally of 2,859 goals (a world record) and 6,001 points scored, he was firmly established in the record books and few were willing to continue the argument. It had been obvious to even the most dim-witted of Rugby League talent scouts that the 6 feet 2-inch and 14-stone full back, who had played a full season for Cardiff at 16 years of age and who was probably the youngest ever Barbarians player at 17, had something special in his rugby repertoire. From his debut for Wigan against Widnes in 1921 until his retirement in 1946 'Sully' was the leading personality in the world of Rugby League, establishing a consistency of play and collecting such a total of points whenever he played that opposing teams would concentrate their whole team plans on stopping him.

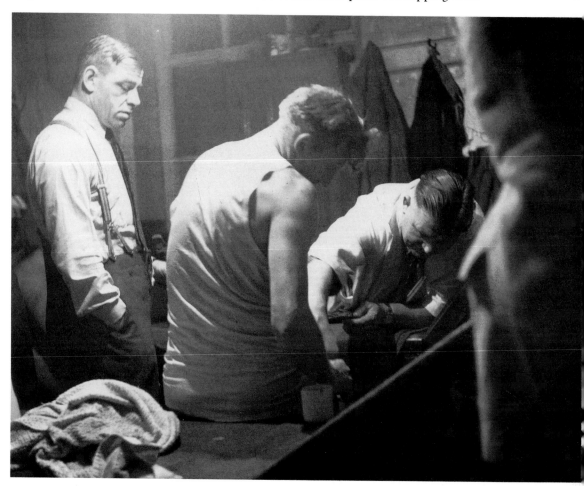

A glance at his achievements will indicate his prowess and his standing above all others in the League code, before or since his arrival in the North. Between 1921 and 1939 Jim topped the goalkicking charts for every season bar two, never once kicking less than 100 goals. In one match for Wigan in a Challenge Cup tie against the amateurs Flimby and Fothergill he kicked 22 goals. At Test level he was to take part in five successive Ashes Test victories and on his three tours to Australia and New Zealand in 1924, 1928 and 1932 (as captain) he punished the men Down Under by amassing 246 goals and four tries. The fans at the Sydney Cricket Ground were sick of him piling up the points and, as one contemporary writer recorded, there was great relief and incredulity if ever he failed:

'On the 1932 Australian tour during a Test match at Sydney Cricket Ground, a little chap who was standing on the famous Hill could not see what was taking place. Suddenly there was a huge cheer and the little man asked someone what had happened. "Jim Sullivan has kicked a goal" was the answer. "Cor," the man replied, "I thought he'd missed from the size of the roar!"'

As a goalkicker Sullivan's accuracy and strength of kick was uncanny and there is no better estimation of his talents than that of his two greatest rivals. Jim Brough admitted: 'He stood alone. In country games [on tour in Australia] where scores were high, some of the players scored as far away from the posts as possible to upset him but it made no difference'. Gus Risman said that he had seen 'none better'.

He possessed a prodigious kick upfield, too, and in the days of kicking duels between opposing full backs (a tactic used to gain ground and to put the opposition in a defensive situation) Jim had the cunning of a fox. When each full back was stationed in his 25 yards area Jim Sullivan would often deliberately shorten his kick to draw his counterpart further upfield, a few yards at a time. He would allow the player's confidence to grow, and then suddenly he would release one of his mighty kicks of the ball to send it rolling into touch 20 yards behind the hapless full back. He was not merely a goalkicker but also a master tactician as captain of Wigan and Great Britain, and a strong-running, attacking full back.

Gus Risman, in his autobiography, explained one of Jim's favourite manoeuvres: 'Every game against him was an education. His favourite tactic was a quick dash up the blind side where he would take two or three tacklers with him, leaving the way clear for a pass to the wing and a clear run to the line.' His effect on the rest of his own players also brought the highest of praise from Gus, himself one of the finest skippers the game has produced: 'The most brilliant captain the game has ever seen, a general willing to do as much work as the privates. He had timing, direction and strength.'

Possessing such a vast array of talent and such an appetite for the game (he made over 922 first class appearances) it is no wonder that,

The clash of the Titans. Jim Sullivan (right), arguably the world's greatest ever full back, meets Rugby Union's finest, Kiwi George Nepia, before Nepia's debut for the now defunct Streatham and Mitcham club in 1935.

following his retirement in 1946, he became an excellent coach with Wigan and St Helens, taking both teams over the next 14 years to some of their most famous triumphs and nurturing some of their greatest players, men of the calibre of Joe Egan, Ken Gee, Alex Murphy and Vince Karalius. If the Australians can refer to their hero, Dally Messenger, as 'The Master', then Jim Sullivan to the British was surely the 'King' of Rugby League.

MICK SULLIVAN

My lasting vision of Mick Sullivan is of him being carried from the field at Swinton at the close of the Challenge Cup semi-final between his Dewsbury side and St Helens in 1966. We had both clashed in a fierce touchline 'altercation', the result of a series of bone-shattering tackles made by both of us throughout a pulsating match in which Mick, then skipper and loose forward of the lowly Yorkshire club, had led Dewsbury to within minutes of a shock Wembley appearance. His raw courage and defiance, his astute rugby brain and ferocious tackling in that match were still instinctive to him, although he was at the end of a great career which had its origins with the Shaw Cross Boys amateur League side in Dewsbury. His career had indeed come full circle.

Mick never asked any favours on the field and, as with me on that eventful day at Swinton, never bore any animosity to the opposition once the game was over. But on the pitch he was the toughest wing I ever played with or against. Although he was barely 5 feet 10 inches tall and tipped the scales at 13 stones, he established himself as one of the best left wingers and the most-capped Great Britain player of all time with 46 appearances between his explosive start in the 1954 World Cup in France and his final Test against Australia in 1963. These were nine tempestuous years of international rugby for this controversial player, who was able to register 40 tries and create a record run of 36 successive international appearances. Mick especially relished his outings against 'th'aud enemy', and was both loved and hated by the fans Down Under. In one particularly hard-fought Test on the 1958 tour, a tour on which he scored a record 38 tries, he aroused the anger and adoration of the crowd on the Sydney Cricket Ground Hill with his typically provocative actions. In the defeat of Australia in a rugged third Test by 40–17, Mick scored a hat trick of tries, became involved in a furious row over an obstruction on an Australian player and was the target for a barrage of missiles from the hostile Aussies. The atmosphere was tense but 'Sully' defused the situation with a touch of his own cheeky brand of humour when he picked up one of the missiles, an orange, peeled it and proceeded to eat it, much to the amusement of the crowd. It was no surprise when Mick Sullivan, at the end of his career in Britain, joined a rebel league in New South Wales, playing for Junee for a season. He relished a challenge.

His career at home took in three of the greatest clubs in the game's history, Huddersfield, Wigan and St Helens, with whom he gained every winner's medal available and for whom he displayed all the skills associated with wing play – speed, swerve, sidestep and a controlled aggression in the tackle which made him the most feared of left wingers. Indeed, genuine left wingers are a rarity in the Rugby League code, for most players prefer to play on the right wing if given the choice, since

b. 12.1.1934
Huddersfield, Wigan,
St Helens, York, Dewsbury,
Junee, Great Britain

their natural inclination is to move off to the right and it is easier to receive the ball from one's left hand side. Alongside Lionel Cooper (Huddersfield), Jack McLean (Bradford Northern) and Alan Edwards (Salford), 'Sully' was more suited to the No. 5 jersey. One of his greatest ploys, so rarely seen in the modern game, was the crash tackle on the opposition centre. Being one of that select group of wingmen which actually relishes tackling, Mick liked nothing better than to wait for the opposition centre to receive the ball before timing his entry inside from the wing to meet the attacker with a sudden crash tackle in which he smothered man and ball to stop any promising move. His timing was perfect and the impact was invariably spectacular, meeting with boos and cheers from the crowd. Mick would greet such clamour with a huge grin, content to be loved or hated wherever he played. Yet I can honestly say there was no more welcome player as a team-mate when the odds were stacked against you, for his professionalism and his sense of humour filled a team with confidence.

The determination shown in Mick Sullivan's touchline dash enabled him to become Great Britain's most-capped player of all time with 46 appearances.

KEVIN TAMATI

Kevin Tamati's sweetest moment in Test rugby came after New Zealand's crushing of Australia in 1985 in the third Test at Carlow Park, Auckland by 18–0. As a celebration of his final appearance in New Zealand at Test level, and in honour of his country stopping the mighty Kangaroos from scoring a single point for the first time in 67 Tests between the two countries, he and his cousin Howie led the jubilant crowd in the Maoris' traditional Haka dance in front of the main grandstand. And how Kevin Tamati deserved the adulation of the crowd after that epic Test match, for it was his seventh attempt to topple the green and gold rugby machine. His performance and the match result were the culmination of a great international career, begun in League only by accident many years before in Wellington.

Having played as a youngster at centre in Union during his schooldays at Hastings, Hawke's Bay, Kevin's introduction to League came about

b. 21.9.1953
Petone, Upper Hutt,
Randwick, Widnes,
Warrington, New Zealand

The exuberant Kiwi forward Kevin Tamati was in his element when battling in the midst of a tough forward exchange.

by sheer chance when he moved home to Wellington. One evening, when attempting to find the Petone Rugby Union Club where he intended to join in a training session, he lost his way and found himself at the doors of the Petone Rugby League Club. Not wishing to waste a training night, he joined the League boys out on the pitch where his handling ability, ball-playing sense and fiercely competitive tackling made him a natural for the League code. Although he eventually found his way to the Upper Hutt and Randwick clubs in Wellington he never again strayed in the direction of a Union club.

The 5 feet 10-inch, 15-stone prop won his first Test cap in 1979 and proved a worthy foe for all opposition over the next seven seasons, not only in the scrum but in the loose, where his mobility enabled him to surprise many a defence with a fine burst of speed. In 1984 I had the pleasure of watching this rugged prop take the award for the Man of the Series in the home Tests against Great Britain. For me, during that season he proved himself the finest prop in the world. Fiercely patriotic, he hunted his opponents as if New Zealand's destiny itself depended upon every tackle made. He led charges in the middle of the field which saw him burst through the brittle ranks of the British defences. And, when through the opposition defence, he could lay off the ball to the backs with the skill and precision of a classy half back.

Kevin's career at club level was crowned by his appearances for Widnes (1982–85) and then Warrington (1985–88) where he won Challenge Cup and Premiership medals. At Warrington he added hooking to his repertoire of skills, when, owing to serious injury problems at Wilderspool, he often took over the No. 9 role with considerable success. His enthusiasm for League has never wavered since his accidental introduction to it at Petone. Now, as the Rugby League's development officer for the Warrington district, he is only too willing to help others enjoy the game, whether they, like Kevin, enter its ranks by accident or not.

JOSEPH THOMPSON

When Joe Thompson played his first game for Leeds in 1923, after signing from the Cross Keys Rugby Union Club, he doubted whether he was suited to the new code. 'So fast was my first game against Huddersfield that I thought I was taking part in a seven-a-side game,' he remembered. Yet by the time of his retirement ten years later he had earned the reputation of one of Leeds' greatest forwards and was the only forward ever to play in three Ashes-winning touring sides in 1924, 1928 and 1932. He was rightly accorded the honour of life membership of the Leeds Rugby League Club for his services to club and country, both on and off the field.

Born at Harnbrook in Gloucestershire, Joe developed into an

b. 22.12.1902
Leeds, Great Britain

Not only a specialist in the art of the close foot dribble, a much favoured tactic in the 1920s, Joe Thompson was also adept at distributing the ball with his hands.

Joe Thompson.

immensely strong yet versatile forward who achieved the unusual distinction of playing at Test level in three positions in the pack – prop, second row and loose forward. He was also one of that long tradition of goalkickers from the forwards. Martin Hodges, Ben Gronow and Harry Bath are examples of big men who kicked the ball between the goalposts with tremendous power. Joe Thompson, with over 1,000 goals to his credit during his career, was among the best of the goalkicking forwards. Only the presence of the master goalkicker, Jim Sullivan, on his three Great Britain trips abroad stopped Joe from being the first choice kicker on tour but, from few opportunities, he did kick 43 goals during his three visits Down Under.

While he was adept at any forward position, Joe Thompson preferred the second row or loose forward spots in that they allowed him to perform a speciality of the 1920s era – the close foot dribble. I remember in my own early Rugby Union days at school being taught how to lead a 'foot rush' down the field by dribbling the ball along the ground with the sides of my rugby boots. We practised this for many hours, almost in the style of soccer players, and the skill was often used to launch an attack, especially on wet, muddy days when opponents experienced great difficulty in falling on the ball or picking it up to stop the movement. The forwards used to take it in turns to dribble the ball whenever one of them overran it. Such an art survived in the League code until the outbreak of the Second World War and Joe Thompson was renowned as the master at wheeling the scrum and emerging with the ball at the toe of his boot. His speed of movement up the field, while dribbling the ball, was so great that it took many a defender by surprise. Such was his skill and the effectiveness of his manœuvre that Joe used to bemoan its decline after the War.

Although he is quite rightly remembered for his deeds on the Headingley pitch in the Leeds colours or on some distant field representing his country, Joe Thompson made a considerable contribution to the code's development off the field. His assistance to the great Jonty Parkin in coaching Jean Galia's French touring team in those pioneer matches in England in 1933 led to the eventual formation of the French Rugby League on Galia's arrival back in France. No doubt Joe tutored them in 'Le Dribble'!

DEREK TURNER

During the 1950s and the 1960s three loose forwards dominated the game: Vince Karalius, John Whiteley and Derek Turner. Each had his own distinctive style of play, none more so than Derek, who well deserved his nickname 'Rocky', which invariably accompanied him wherever he played. Short and squat like his namesake, the heavyweight world champion boxer 'Rocky' Marciano, he was just as tough and uncompromising on the pitch as Marciano was to his opponents in the ring. 'Rocky' Turner was not as fast as his other two rivals but he was supreme in the close midfield work of the forwards and his tackle was exceptionally hard and effective. He relished the hard forward battles and his captaincy of three Wembley cup-winning sides bears testimony to his rugged qualities, as he was especially suited to the Cup rounds played in the harsh, wintry conditions of January and February.

His performance in defeat, when playing with Wakefield Trinity against St Helens in the first round of the Challenge Cup in 1966, was indicative of his never-say-die spirit. Playing in the front row of the pack, a position he took up later in his career, he was felled in a strong tackle which caused him to break his collar bone. He knew the battle was at a crucial point with both sides locked in midfield, each seeking the one try which might tip the balance in their favour. That St Helens, thanks to a Tommy Bishop try, struck first and went on to win is history, but it was only when all hope had gone for Trinity that 'Rocky' Turner retired from the field leaving his colleagues to battle on without him. He was certainly a man of great courage and endeavour.

Derek was the ideal tough forward for Test match rugby, where defence is the first priority of a forward and one is expected never to take a step back. He represented his country in the World Cup of 1957 and was a model tourist in 1962, going on to win 24 caps for Great Britain while at Oldham and Wakefield Trinity.

It is more than coincidence that great players tend to play for great sides; the two, player and team, tend to come together naturally. And there is no doubt that when he moved from Hull Kingston Rovers to Oldham in the 1956–59 period, he played with one of the finest club teams I have ever seen. Indeed, the pack of Don Vines, Jack Keith, Ken Jackson, Sid Little, Charlie Winslade and Derek Turner was a frightening prospect to behold as they went about their work. His move to Wakefield Trinity in 1959 for a transfer fee of £8,000 also coincided with the rise of a great era for Trinity in which, alongside Neil Fox, Harold Poynton and Gerry Round he won every trophy available to the club. Derek's fighting qualities and strong leadership not only stood him in good stead as a player but helped him to enjoy considerable success as a coach with Castleford and then Leeds.

b. 18.11.1932
Hull Kingston Rovers,
Oldham, Wakefield Trinity,
Great Britain

OVERLEAF: *A jubilant Derek Turner is hoisted aloft by his Trinity pack team-mates, Jack Wilkinson (left) and Don Vines, after skippering Wakefield to a record victory, 38–5, over Hull in the 1960 Challenge Cup final.*

203

DAVE VALENTINE

Dave Valentine's greatest moment in an outstanding rugby career at both League and Union was surely when he was chaired from the field in 1954 at the Parc des Princes Stadium in Paris as the successful skipper of Great Britain's World Cup-winning team. This World Cup final play-off, in which Britain defeated France 16–12 before a wildly enthusiastic crowd of over 30,000 was the vindication of the young 'no hopers' and a tribute to the experience of their captain, who had moulded them into a team barely two months after he himself had returned home from an exhaustive Lions tour of Australia and New Zealand. It was perhaps fitting that his fellow Scots, David Rose and Gordon Brown, should score the crucial tries.

b. 12.9.1926
Huddersfield, Great Britain

Dave Valentine will always be remembered for his captaincy of the victorious Great Britain side for the 1954 World Cup, previously dismissed as 'no hopers'.

David, a black haired, craggy ex-Hawick and Scotland Union player, revealed all the qualities we associate with Scottish Rugby Union back row forward play. He had pace, a safe pair of hands, a nimble and far-seeing rugby brain and that rugged approach to tackling which is encouraged in the Border Country. He led by example, always in the thick of midfield pack skirmishes, but he was a thinker on the game who liked to indulge in open play with the backs. To add to his two Union caps he won 15 League caps while at Huddersfield, where he was part of that famous post-War team which, from 1948 to 1954, contained such stars as Lionel Cooper, John Hunter, Peter Henderson and Pat Devery. As the loose forward supreme, he and his pack provided the opportunities for such back stars to flourish.

Although Huddersfield have in the past encouraged Scottish Union converts to join them, notably players like centre Alex Fiddes and flying wing Jock Anderson, it is strange that Scotland has proved such a barren hunting ground for the Rugby League talent scouts over the years. Since the breakaway in 1895 by the Northern Union from the Rugby Football Union 148 Welsh Union internationals and countless club players have trekked north, but only 14 Scottish Union internationals have crossed Hadrian's Wall and precious few club players. Rugby Union in Scotland is essentially the preserve of the independent schools sector, not normally a productive area for potential League players, but when one considers the talent of players such as George Fairbairn (ex-Kelso), Ron Cowan (ex-Selkirk), Brian Shillinglaw (ex-Gala) and Dave Valentine himself, then perhaps it is time that we turned our attentions further north.

In later life Dave Valentine was to become a successful coach with the Huddersfield Rugby League Club, but he remained a lover of both codes of rugby and was always prepared to help out when his talents were needed. During a spell in the mid-1970s, when I was secretly coaching Rugby Union at St Helens, I arrived at the Huddersfield Union club for a match and, not wishing to cause any embarrassment to our opponents on account of my League background, I sidled unobtrusively to the side of the club pavilion. To my surprise, I bumped into Dave Valentine who, having confessed that he was coaching the Yorkshire side, invited me in for a pre-match drink. The true spirit of rugby for either code!

TOM VAN VOLLENHOVEN

The history of South African Rugby Union players enjoying a career in Rugby League is a long and colourful one. From the 1920s, when Adrian Van Heerdon and George Van Rooyen played with distinction, to the present-day contributions of Ray Mordt and Rob Louw at Wigan, the ex-Springboks have invariably adapted well to League. Of all the imports, however, none can compare with St Helens' prize capture in 1957 – Tom Van Vollenhoven, a winger who was to electrify the crowds wherever he played. And yet he so nearly did not play for the Saints.

The 22-year-old Springbok wing had proved a sensation for South Africa in the Test series against the British Lions Rugby Union side in 1955 and he continued his amazing deeds while touring Australia and New Zealand a year later. He was able to sprint 100 yards in 9.8 seconds and could beat men with ease along the touchlines. It was no surprise that he attracted the attentions of George Duckworth, the ex-Lancashire wicketkeeper who was on tour with the England cricket XI. His reports

b. 29.4.1935
St Helens

Legendary Springbok flyer Tom Van Vollenhoven came to the rescue of St Helens and myself on countless occasions, electrifying the crowds wherever he went.

filtered through to both Wigan and St Helens, provoking a hectic chase for his signature in June and July 1957. A fee of £4,000 secured his services for St Helens. However, Wigan missed his signature only by a matter of minutes because a telegram boy, carrying another huge financial offer to Tom, had to stop at the side of the road to mend a puncture on his bicycle. That delay proved a stroke of divine intervention for Saints, who wasted little time in transferring him to Knowsley Road for his home debut on 26th October against Leeds before a crowd of some 23,000 spectators. His second match, an 'A' team fixture against Whitehaven, drew a record 'A' team crowd of 8,500 and prompted the highly respected Rugby League journalist, Keith Macklin, to write: 'He shot into his stride as if catapulted from an ejector seat, leaving three men clutching air and trailing in his wake as he flashed around the posts'. Tom Van Vollenhoven had truly arrived and Keith Macklin's words were to be repeated in varying forms over the next ten seasons until Tom's retirement in 1968.

Having played alongside Tom Van Vollenhoven for St Helens and also in a tour trial match prior to the 1968 World Cup, I was privileged to watch his talents at close quarters. His selection for that tour trial enabled him to be the only South African to wear a Great Britain jersey and was a fitting tribute to his impact on the sport. His speed was that of a pure athlete and his acceleration was such that, even in a friendly game of touch rugby in training, he could receive the ball while standing still opposite you and yet be past before you could move towards him. After this sudden acceleration he could cruise at top speed for the full length of the touchline. He was immensely strong in the thighs and upper body and, weighing about $13\frac{1}{2}$ stones, he could break through any tackles if he wished. However, like all classical wingers he preferred to use his body swerve or sidestep. In defence he was, unlike many wingers, a keen tackler, and such an instinctive footballer that he could play in the centre position whenever needed. He was a rugby genius!

Tom Van Vollenhoven's initial fee of £4,000 looked like small change when set, ten years later, against his tryscoring feats for St Helens. His total of 62 tries in season 1958–59 is still the club record today, as is his scoring of six tries in an individual match, a feat which he achieved against Wakefield Trinity (1957) and Blackpool Borough (1962) respectively. He registered 397 tries for St Helens in his ten-year League career, scoring none better than his tries in the Challenge Cup final of 1961 and the Championship final of 1959, which helped his team-mates gain winners' medals against Wigan and Hunslet, and exhibited every facet of his many skills. His 90-yard interpassing movement with centre Ken Large at Wembley illustrated his sheer pace, balance and body swerve, while his 75-yard try against Hunslet in the Championship final highlighted his strength, sidestep, hand-off and rugby sense. That try, in which he beat four men without veering more than two yards from the touchline, should be shown to all aspiring wingers.

HAROLD WAGSTAFF

The 'Prince of Centres' as Harold Wagstaff, the Huddersfield and Great Britain tour captain of 1914 and 1920, was known, stood head and shoulders above anyone in the League code in the first 30 years of the breakaway from Rugby Union. Few since have matched his skills as a centre threequarter and perhaps none has been blessed with the same inspirational powers of leadership. Mr V. Beanland, in his book *Great Games and Great Players* published in 1945, declared that: 'It was his scheming brain that made him the great player that he was. Wagstaff fitted quietly and unostentatiously into his side and if you watched him closely you would realise how perfectly he blended in with his colleagues, how obviously he was the "god in the machine", how deep was his knowledge of the weaknesses of the opposition and how amazing was his intuition as to the right thing to do at the right moment'.

It was obvious at an early stage in his rugby life that Harold Wagstaff was special. Signed by the famous Huddersfield club from the local Underbank amateurs for five gold sovereigns, a princely sum in those days, he became one of the youngest ever professional players when he pulled on the claret and gold jersey for his first match at Bramley, on 10th November 1906, at the amazingly tender age of 15 years and 175 days. County honours with Yorkshire and an international cap were awarded to him before he was 18. Sadly, the war years restricted his number of Test caps to nine, but they did not stop him from being the leader of one of the greatest teams in the history of Rugby League and the architect of perhaps the most famous Test victory in the history of the Anglo/Australian Ashes series.

With international forwards Duggie Clark and Ben Gronow providing the possession, the Huddersfield threequarter line at the time of the First World War carried all before it. Harold Wagstaff was the creative spirit alongside the undoubted skills of Rosenfeld, Gleeson and Moorhouse, who between them scored over 200 tries in one season and who, during Wagstaff's career with the team at Fartown from 1906 to 1925, helped him to lift every trophy available. It was with that 'Team of all Talents', as the Yorkshiremen were known, that he developed his fine understanding of men and gained the ability to inspire others, characteristics which were to help him gain victory at Test level despite seemingly incredible odds.

As captain on the 1914 Lions tour Harold, having abided by the Australians' requirements to play two Test matches within three days, was naturally upset when he was instructed to play a third Test five days later. To make matters worse he was hard pressed to raise a team due to numerous injuries. Politics, however, entered the fray and, as Wagstaff remembered, 'A special meeting of the Northern Union Council was called. They agreed to the Australian demand and sent the

b. 19.5.1891
Huddersfield, Great Britain

Harold Wagstaff and his Huddersfield 'Team of all Talents' dominated the Rugby League scene during the first 30 years following the breakaway from Union.

following message to the British party in Australia. "Play match as Australians desire. England expects that every man will do his duty"! So it came about that the third Test was played on the Saturday following the first – three Tests in eight days for a touring team crippled by injury!'

That Great Britain won 14–6, despite being down to ten players after only 50 minutes play, speaks volumes for Harold Wagstaff's powers of leadership and the courage of his players. The match has justifiably passed into Rugby League legend as the 'Rorke's Drift Test'. Harold recalled how his team fought a rearguard action against incredible odds. 'My first memory of the day on which the match was played has to do with the fighting speech that was made to us by Mr Clifford [the manager]. He said that he expected every one of us to play as we had never played before. "You are playing in a game of football this afternoon, but more than that, you're playing for England" ... Ten men and 30 minutes to go! But never had I nine such men with me on a football field as I had that day. We were in our half all the time, and for most of it we seemed to be on our line, but we stuck it. Our forwards gave their all. But victory was ours. When the whistle sounded we were done. We had gone to the last gasp and were just about finished.'

ERNEST WARD

Ernest Ward, the Bradford Northern and Great Britain captain of the 1950 Lions tour, was once described by Harry Sunderland, a former Australian tour manager and radio commentator, as 'a graceful centre threequarter. England has never sent us a more calm, good mannered, well conducted player'. Ernest deserved every attribute described by Harry Sunderland. As a youngster, I was allowed by my father to miss just one afternoon of my schooling when I accompanied him over the Pennines on an old rickety double-decker council bus from St Helens to Odsal Stadium, Bradford to watch our beloved Saints attempt to topple the mighty Northern team. I was given instructions to watch Ernest Ward, the peerless centre who was to skipper them to three successive Wembley finals, 1947–49, and to learn from him.

At 6 feet and 13½ stones this slimly built centre was a classical player, precise in everything he did, rarely stooping to illegal play. A gentleman on and off the field, he was a pure footballer with a fine turn of speed and an eye for an opening but, above all, he timed his passes beautifully.

b. 30.7.1920
Bradford Northern, Castleford, Batley, Great Britain

Ernest Ward, an accomplished goalkicker as well as a creative, tryscoring centre, turns away confidently after a successful attempt at goal in Great Britain's second Test against Australia in 1948.

Ernest Ward.

He was a winger's delight, rarely releasing the ball until he had man-œuvred his wing partner into a better position than himself. He was a tactician and was never afraid to risk a long, raking, touch-finding kick upfield to relieve pressure on his team or to force an attacking position.

Such qualities naturally led to him being selected for both the 1946 and 1950 Lions tours, the latter as captain, and being asked to represent his country on 20 occasions in Test matches against Australia or New Zealand. Nor was he merely a creative player, for his career tally of 862 goals and 151 tries and his tour record of 17 goals against Mackay in 1946 prove that he was as hungry as most threequarters to score points.

Ernest was especially proud of his rugby record in wartime, when a special dispensation was given to players of both codes, League and Union, to take part together in special Armed Services charity matches under Union rules. He excelled as the captain and full back of the England side which included two secretaries who, later in life, were to serve the Rugby Football Union with such distinction – Robin Prescott and Bob Weighill.

Signed as a 16-year-old for the sum of £150 from Dewsbury Boys club in 1936, he represented Bradford Northern, and later Castleford as player-coach for two seasons, with distinction for 20 years. Although Ernest won every honour in the game, including the Lance Todd Trophy as the Man of the Match in Northern's defeat of Halifax in the 1949 Challenge Cup final, his contributions to the welfare of League off the field were immense. The two loves of his life were his position as Chairman of the British Rugby League Lions Association, in which guise he organised many charitable and social functions, and his founding of the Bradford Northern Past Players' Association. I well remember the tears in his eyes as he sat alongside me at the launch of the ex-players' inaugural dinner in 1987, sadly only a few months before he died.

DAVID WATKINS

To appreciate the intense rugby atmosphere in Blaina one needs to play on the Cwmcelyn Park pitch, perched high alongside a coaltip, as I once did for the Universities Athletic Rugby Union side and as David Watkins did as a youngster before he went on to 21 appearances for Wales. The stocky Welsh fly half was moulded into a great player at an early age while playing schoolboy rugby, cherishing the dream of playing for Wales. At that time he cannot have known that he would become a household name in the code which is spoken of in hushed tones in the Union-mad valleys. His signing for Salford on 19th October 1967 was sensational and his impact over the next 13 seasons, firstly with Salford and then with Swinton, was such that he repaid his £16,000 fee many times over in sheer entertainment value.

b. 5.3.1942
Salford, Swinton, Great Britain

Ex-Wales Rugby Union stand off David Watkins repaid his fee of £16,000, then a world record, many times over, not least with his world goalkicking record of 221 goals in a season in 1972–73.

He was so tense and nervous at the dramatic nature of his decision to sign for the Salford club that he could not eat his meal at the signing venue, The Royal Hop Pole Hotel: 'I sat at the table in the dining room with an empty plate in front of me while the others ate their lunch'. On his debut before a 14,000 crowd at the Willows, Salford he was decidedly shaky, yet he was to become the jewel in the crown of a great Salford era. Further signings by Salford's gifted Chairman, Brian Snape, ensured that players of the quality of Maurice Richards, Chris Hesketh, Mike Coulman and Keith Fielding were gathered to produce a brand of free-flowing rugby not seen at Salford since the days of the famous 'Red Devils' team led by Gus Risman in the 1930s.

Although David was awarded only two Great Britain Rugby League caps, against New Zealand in 1971 and Australia in 1974, this should not belittle his mercurial talents and outstanding contribution to the League code. His speed off the mark was most disconcerting to any slow, lumbering forward and his instinct for a gap when linking up from full back or when attacking from his stand off role was uncanny. At a time when tactical kicking was on the wane, David Watkins resurrected it as a weapon in Salford's armoury. There was no finer sight than David pinning a side back near their own try line with one of his long, flighted kicks to touch. But it is his appetite for points for which he will always be remembered.

His 100 goals in 18 matches in 1972–73 is still a League record, shared with Bernard Ganley and Steve Quinn. His world goalkicking record of 221 goals in that same season will probably stand for many years to come, especially as there are now fewer opportunities of taking a kick at goal because of the differential penalty. But his record for the longest scoring run, playing and scoring in 92 consecutive matches for Salford, is the record which epitomises for me his appetite and aptitude for Rugby League. It is a hard sport, and for one as small as David Watkins to shrug off the bumps and bruises and escape the close attention that he suffered in those 92 matches between 19th August 1972 and 25th April 1974 is little short of the incredible. That he scored a total of 403 goals, 41 tries and 929 points says much for his unique skills.

Having given magnificent service to Salford until the age of 37, David Watkins enjoyed two further seasons with Salford's deadly rivals, Swinton, before attempting to revive the League code in Wales with a venture at Cardiff. Sadly, despite tempting Welsh Union stars like Steve Fenwick, Tom David and Paul Ringer to join the Cardiff Blue Dragons and despite much hard work on David's part, circumstances were not right for success and the enterprise was aborted. David Watkins' appetite for rugby did not suffer however and he has since carved out another successful career as a radio and television commentator on Rugby League matches.

CLIFF WATSON

When St Helens placed an advertisement in a national daily newspaper for 'big, strong men to consider playing Rugby League', little did the Board of Directors ever imagine that their novel enterprise would be rewarded by the capture of one of Great Britain's finest and toughest prop forwards. Cliff Watson, a 16-stone, Cockney-born prop from the tiny Dudley-Kingswinford Rugby Union Club in the Midlands, decided to try his luck and, after a couple of 'A' team trials and a mere handful of first team games, he was the subject of rapturous applause for his try-saving cover tackle on Wigan wing Billy Boston in the 1961 Challenge Cup final at Wembley. He had signed for St Helens in August 1960, but he announced his arrival on the Rugby League scene on that warm sunny day in May and was rarely out of the spotlight until his departure in 1971 to join Cronulla in Sydney.

b. 26.4.1940
St Helens, Cronulla,
Wollongong, Great Britain

The 1966 Cup final, in which St Helens met Wigan. St Helens' Cliff Watson meets Prime Minister Harold Wilson under the scrutiny of yours truly in the foreground.

215

Cliff was an immensely strong prop whose speciality, under the old unlimited tackle rule in operation until 1966 which allowed a team to retain possession until an offence was created, was to drive the ball away from his own line. Despite lacking a finger on one hand he would grip the ball tightly and force his way through the fiercest of attempted tackles, race upfield and set an attack in motion. When I played alongside him in the St Helens team of the 1960s he would take up a defensive position on one side of the play the ball and I would take up a position on the other side. It was interesting how much tackling I had to do as few players seemed to relish running in the direction of Cliff's all-consuming 'bear hug' tackle. With a fine sense of humour, he was an indispensable player to any coach wanting to develop that vital ingredient of successful sides: team spirit.

Cliff's performances both on and off the field made him a key member of the 1966 tour of Australia and the 1968 World Cup party which travelled to both Australia and New Zealand. His sterling efforts at prop in the Test series of 1970 on the Lions tour of Australia helped the team to win the Ashes. His performances Down Under attracted the attentions of the Sydney clubs and in particular of Tommy Bishop, his old St Helens team-mate, then the player-coach of Cronulla. His signing for Cronulla in 1971 coincided with the club's most successful period as he and Bishop helped to lift the club from near the bottom of the Sydney League table to the Sydney Grand Final against Manly in 1973. His playing career was concluded at the junior club of Wollongong where, as player-coach, he passed on the benefit of his considerable experience to younger players.

It is amusing to marvel in these days of specialist diets and nutritional advice for our leading sportsmen that Cliff Watson ever managed to take the field, such was his appetite before a game. Not for Cliff the lightly boiled egg on toast or the medium rare steak. No, he preferred a full four-course lunch, often less than an hour before kick-off, and extra portions of chips were always welcome. Yet his energy never wavered and he was the fittest forward I ever had the pleasure of playing alongside.

GRAEME WEST

Standing alongside this ex-Kiwi Test captain, at 6 feet 5 inches the tallest man ever to play in a Challenge Cup final at Wembley, one might be forgiven for thinking that he would have made a magnificent second row for the All Black Union side. And, but for a change of employment, he was surely destined to play alongside All Black great Graham Mourie, his Union team-mate in Taranaki's Under 15 side.

Despite a strong family background in the Union code, which included an uncle who represented the All Blacks 1924 touring side known as 'The Invincibles', Graeme switched allegiance when, on becoming a slaughterman, he came under the influence of his boss, Barry Giltrap. In Hawera Graeme developed such a commitment to the League code that by 1972 he and his boss had introduced League to the township of Stretford and, having scored two tries on his League debut, he soon set his sights on a successful League career. Although he made his international debut in the 1975 World Cup tournament, it was not until 1979 that he captained his country against Great Britain in two Tests.

Both Graeme West and Mark Graham, another New Zealand Test captain, are unusually tall for Rugby League forwards. As they are expected to perform far more running, passing and handling than their counterparts in Union, most League forwards tend to be around the 6-feet mark, there being little need for the extra inches needed for line-out play. Graeme West is the exception but, unlike many players of his height in the Union code who lack athleticism and mobility, he has never lacked pace or handling ability. Indeed his huge frame has often been his biggest asset when allied to his sharp rugby brain.

In the modern era of forwards most of our international pack stars have not had the bulk of their predecessors of the 1950s and 1960s when the unlimited tackle rule created the need for very big men. Nonetheless, the sheer size of Graeme enabled him to remain upright in the tackle and still pass the ball to colleagues in support. When taking the ball at first receiver he was able to scatter half-hearted tacklers and pass the ball on to the speedier forwards in support. Whether at second row or prop Graeme always played the full 80 minutes, setting an example to others with his sense of leadership. It was essentially for those qualities that Wigan secured his signature on a £60,000 five-year playing contract in 1982. Under the coaching of Alex Murphy and later under his great mentor, fellow countryman Graham Lowe, Graeme played his full part as skipper in raising the Central Park club to pre-eminence in world club rugby.

The Rugby League novice, who once scored six tries for Taranaki against Wellington, developed into a fine captain at Wigan, experiencing no greater pleasure than holding aloft the Silk Cut Challenge Cup in

b. 5.12.1953
Hawera, Taranaki, Wigan,
New Zealand

1985 after Wigan beat Hull 28–24 in an enthralling match. A further thrill for the powerful Kiwi was the knowledge that he was only the second New Zealand player to captain a winning side at Wembley since his former coach, Cec Mountford, skippered the same club 24 years previously.

Coated with mud from the hard forward contests he relished, a delighted Graeme West emerges from the fray to celebrate Wigan's 1984 Challenge Cup semi-final win over York.

DES WHITE

Des White, the Auckland and New Zealand full back between 1950 and 1956, was a strong runner with the ball, a fearless tackler and a shrewd tactician yet, surprisingly, he will be best remembered as the greatest points-scorer and goalkicker New Zealand ever had. He was the scourge of all opposition during his 61 appearances in a Kiwi jersey.

b. 16.2.1927
Auckland, New Zealand

For the first 80 years of the League code's existence it had been the traditional role of a full back to be the team's goalkicker. As well as his usual role of kicking to touch, the full back, if he ever hoped to gain international honours, had to be an accurate goalkicker. Each era has thrown up a succession of first class full backs who were also accomplished goalkickers. Jim Sullivan and Jim Brough, Bernard Ganley and Geoff Pimblett, Mick Burke and Steve Hesford are names which readily spring to mind. And yet, in the modern era, rule changes, notably the inclusion of the differential penalty for offences which were once punishable by the opportunity to kick at goal, and changing styles of play have seen the demise of the goalkicking full back. Indeed, two of the best in the world, Garry Jack (Balmain and Australia) and Steve Hampson (Wigan and Great Britain), rarely attempt a kick at goal. But in the 1950s the first requirement of a full back, and the major reason

Auckland and New Zealand full back Des White was the scourge of international Rugby League in the 1950s with his uncanny knack of running up points.

for his inclusion in a Test team, was the ability to kick goals. Little wonder then that Auckland's Des White was the first name pencilled into the Kiwis' team sheet. In six seasons of international rugby he rewrote the New Zealand record books.

In 61 appearances he landed 223 goals, including a record 63 goals in 21 Tests. He also added seven tries to his goalscoring feats bringing him a record 467 points in internationals. Des White's feats in individual Test matches and Test series also took his name into the record books. Seven goals in the second Test at Greymouth between New Zealand and Great Britain in 1954 gave him the record for the highest number of goals scored by a Kiwi against Great Britain. He performed even better against Australia in amassing 11 goals in the second Test match of the 1952 series at Sydney Cricket Ground. In the same series he scored a record 36 points for New Zealand in a Test series against Australia. He was also the first Kiwi to top a century of points on an overseas tour with 107 points during that 1952 visit to Australia.

Goalkicking is an art, often practised to perfection after many hours spent alone propelling a ball in the direction of the posts. To be successful at international level, when the pressure is at its most intense, the kicker must have nerves of steel and the utmost confidence in himself. Des White had just that.

JOHN WHITELEY

A Rugby Union convert's opening matches are usually nerve-racking, frenetic affairs with the League novice eager to gain as much advice and experience as he can from his new team colleagues and even from the opposition. How well I remember a last ditch tackle of mine on Hull loose forward John Whiteley as he strode down the middle of the field towards our try line. With seconds of the match remaining, I scythed him down with what I thought was a copybook tackle around the ankles. The final whistle sounded and John Whiteley rose from the floor saying, 'That was a good tackle, Ray. But you'll have to learn to tackle the forwards a little higher so as to clamp the ball and stop them passing'. Where others might have been angry or frustrated at not scoring the match-winning try, John took the time to give me, the new convert to Rugby League, some very sensible advice. He was a true gentleman.

This 6 feet 2-inch and 15-stone product of the Hull Boys' club was a great athlete, superbly fit and an exceptionally skilful passer of the ball. If you allowed John Whiteley any freedom with his arms they would stretch out of the tackle, around his opponent, to deliver the neatest of defence-splitting passes. In attack, he liked nothing better than to race down the field, linking up with his threequarters and often testing them for speed. He was one of the 'old school' of loose forwards

b. 20.11.1930
Hull, Great Britain

Hull's John Whiteley adopts the classic loose forward's position at the side of the scrum, halting the progress of Wigan scrum half Rees Thomas. Whiteley's defensive qualities could not prevent Wigan's 30–13 win in the 1959 Challenge Cup final.

who had learned his trade around the base of the scrum and knew how to link with his scrum half. I saw him score one try in a Test match against Australia at Headingley in 1959 which was a perfect combination of loose forward and half back play. His scrum half that day, Jeff Stevenson of Leeds, combined beautifully with him at the base of the scrum, split the Australian midfield defence wide open and allowed John Whiteley to score beneath the posts. Sadly, such combination play around the scrum is not as regularly seen under the new rules, which have led to a fall in the number of scrums and changes in the style of loose forward play.

Although he was a one-club man, never leaving Hull's Boulevard ground, John's talents were recognised internationally and it was not long after his debut with Hull, at the start of the 1950–51 season, that further honours came his way. The 1954 World Cup was to prove the training ground for his apprenticeship as a Great Britain loose forward when, as reserve to skipper Dave Valentine, he joined the successful Great Britain tour to Australia and New Zealand in 1958. His 15 international appearances for Great Britain between 1957 and 1962 were no fewer than John Whiteley deserved.

He surely deserved a better fate than to be the coach of the Great Britain side which was pitted against the invincible Australian team of 1982 in a series that changed the whole of our thinking on the British game. At the time of Great Britain's lowest ebb in international competition I can well remember the look of surprise and anguish on John Whiteley's face when he found that some of his forwards, due to face the Australians that week, could not beat him in a lap around the field. It was a far cry from the fitness levels demanded by John in his own playing days with Great Britain.